A BOOK OF THE MAGI

Lore, Prayers, and Spellcraft of the Three Holy Kings

I0388426

¹ Now when Jesus was born in Bethlehem of Judaea, in the dayes of Herod the king, behold there came Wisemen from the East to Ierusalem,

² Saying, Where is he that is borne king of the Jewes? for we haue seen his star in the East, and are come to worship him.

³ When Herod the king had heard these things, he was troubled, and all Hierusalem with him.

⁴ And when hee had gathered all the chief Priests and Scribes of the people together, hee demanded of them where Christ should be borne.

⁵ And they said unto him, In Bethlehem of Iudaea: for thus it is written by the Prophet,

⁶ And thou Bethlehem, in the land of Iuda, art not the least among the Princes of Iuda: for out of thee shall come a Gouernor, that shall rule my people Israel.

⁷ Then Herod when hee had priuily called the Wisemen, enquired of them diligently what time the Starre appeared.

⁸ And he sent them to Bethlehem, and said, Goe, and search diligently for the yong child, and when ye have found him, bring mee word againe, that I may come and worship him also.

⁹ When they had heard the king, they departed; and, loe, the Starre, which they saw in the East, went before them, till it came: and stood ouer where the yong child was.

¹⁰ When they saw the Starre, they rejoyced with exceeding great joy.

¹¹ And when they were come into the house: they saw the yong child with Mary his mother, and fell downe, and worshipped him: and when they had opened their treasures, they presented vnto him gifts, golde, and frankincense and myrrhe.

¹² And being warned of God in a dream that they should not return to Herod, they departed into their owne countrey another way.

The Gospel of Matthew: 1–12

¹⁰ The kings of Tarshish and of the Isles shall bring presents: the kings of Sheba and Seba shall offer gifts.

¹¹ Yea, all kings shall fall downe before him: all nations shall serve him.

¹² For he shall deliuer the needy when he cryeth; the poore also, and him that hath no helper.

¹³ He shall spare the poor and needy, and shall saue the soules of the needy.

Psalm 72: 10–13
The Holy Bible (London, 1619)

A BOOK
OF MAGI
THE

*Lore, Prayers, and Spellcraft
of the Three Holy Kings*

Alexander Cummins, PhD

Folk Necromancy in Transmission Vol. 3

REVELORE PRESS
Seattle
2018

A Book of the Magi:
Lore, Prayers, and Spellcraft of the Three Holy Kings
© Alexander Cummins 2018.

Third volume of the *Folk Necromancy in Transmission* series
conceived and curated by Dr Alexander Cummins and Jesse Hathaway Diaz.

All rights reserved. No part of this publication may be
reproduced or utilized in any form or by any means, electronic
or mechanical, including photocopying, recording, or by any
information storage and retrieval system, without permission
in writing from the Publishers.

Book design, cover design, & interior figures by Joseph Uccello.
Cover image by S. Aldarnay.

ISBN 978-1-947544-06-2
Printed globally on demand through IngramSpark.

First printed by Revelore Press in 2018.

Revelore Press
220 2nd Ave S #91
Seattle, WA 98104
United States

www.revelore.press

Table of Contents

Acknowledgements	9
Introduction	12

PART I:
THE CULT OF THE MAGI

The Day of Epiphany	17
The Coming of the Kings	20
The Three Holy Kings of Cologne	26
Star Singers	38
Procession, Plays, Pageantry, and Protest	43
Towards a Nigromancy of the Magi	49

PART II:
WORKS OF THE THREE HOLY KINGS

The Cakes of the Kings	54
Prayers to the Three Kings	61
A Work of Healing	65
The Grimoiric Record	66
Workings of Strength and Endurance	67
A Work of Detection	72
Works of Protection	75
Works of Conjuration	81
The Three Kings in the 'Treatise Sion'	88
A Work of Dominating Authorities	94
Works of Adoration	95

Conclusions	109
Bibliography	111
Further Works	114
About this Series	114
About the Author	115
About this Volume	115

Acknowledgements

Thanks should certainly begin with my publisher and collaborator, Dr Jennifer Zahrt, who helped see this book to fruition, from a niggling sense that I should write *something* on this important part of my work and practice to the volume before you. I am excited to continue working at Revelore Press in my capacity as (co-)editor of the Folk Necromancy in Transmission series, and I hope this is a worthy addition to a roster of texts on which I am already very proud to have worked.

I would like to thank my friends and colleagues who proofed this text—especially Nick Grossenbacher—as well as those who read through it and offered feedback, such as J. F., Matthew Venus, and others. I look forward to returning the favour one day!

I am also especially grateful to my friend and colleague Daniel Harms for working his librarian magic to track down, scan and send to me a couple of the source materials contained in this book. I hope to be able to repay him in kind one day.

Thanks for a gorgeous book design itself go to Joseph Uccello, who as always has worked wonders with what we've given him; and to my dear friend and colleague the occult consultant and magical artist S. Aldarnay for our magnificent icon of the Three Holy Kings and the images, seals, and characters within these pages.

I would like especially to thank my godbrothers Demetrius Lakwa, Peter Leykam, and Phillip English for their considered, wise, and generous conversation on this book and so many other matters, and for their unwavering support and encouragement. Three kings, indeed.

I am profoundly grateful to my circle of brilliant, kind, and beautiful friends with whom I have ranted, raved, and worried at about this project: Julio Ody, Rebecca Minchew Stanford, Sam Block, William Koch, Joseph Peterson, Jess Bernhard, Albo Sudekum, Vanessa Irena, Naomi Kashinsky, Stefan Mohammed, Raphael Attar, Leia von Hessen, Matt Barclay, Alkistis Dimech. Peter Grey, Cooper Wilhelm, Jason Miller, Jake Stratton-Kent, and many many many more. Thank you all.

My deepest gratitudes to that rough Goat Jesse Hathaway Diaz for all the absolute everythings; and for his thoughts, conversation, and detailed notes and suggestions on this book; and for being my co-conspirator on Folk Necromancy, and my co-host at Radio Free Golgotha; and for being Best Man. Hekua Baba! Salve Tatá!

To my father Mike, my mother Anne, and my sister Harriet for never letting me forget they are proud of me. Finally, and absolutely most importantly of all, all my love, admiration, and gratitude to my sweetheart, my Star, my best friend, my wife-twice-over Mallorie Vaudoise for the unending rivers of her love, patience, and support. Team. x

I dedicate this book to dead magicians.

INTRODUCTION

The Three Kings. Yes, the Three Kings in the Nativity scenes, displays, and Italian *precepe*. Los Tres Reyes who parade the streets in carnival floats and on camels—for whom good little girls and boys leave out hay or grass before they go to bed, awaiting their gifts from the Magi. The Hispanic Santas. It may at first seem a little ridiculous or perhaps even somewhat contrarian to suggest there is magical (indeed, necromantic) value to a familiar Christmas trope, but I would remind you how much a *very big deal* los Tres Reyes play in Hispanic culture: not simply in the parades and processions, or the foodways and festivities, but in customs, in identity, and in pride. This is not to compare what I am attempting to explore in this text and the centuries of the history of Christendom and colonialism that led to this—but merely to point out the Three Kings are already deeply magical to many, many peoples around the world.

I invite you to ponder potentials for deeper significances of the Magi, and their journey and their Adoration. These figures—somewhat unique in the Bible as heathen magician-kings who are also admirably wise—can be worked as a stable port in and trade route through a swirling sea of Spirit, figureheads with banners ribboning into the winds, by which powerful spirits may be gathered and cohered.

This is a text informed by a nigromancy of a particular

INTRODUCTION

set of ghosts: the shades of deceased magical practitioners. Gathered by a Star in the East, these tutelary spirits can be worked by the light of this Star, and by the virtues imparted by the patronage of the names Caspar, Balthazar, and Melchior.

The Three Kings received real historical cultus—most centrally at the church in Cologne in which their bones were brought to rest, and in the political magian plays of the Medici and other (usually Southern) European cities—but I should be clear: this book includes both historical research and poetic inspiration with my own folk necromantic experiments, ritual devotion, and working of the Magi. I will, however, be at pains to distinguish established historical practices and my own innovations and experiments—for to confuse the two is folly at best, and always a betrayal of the traditions one purports to proffer and celebrate. After surveying some foundational concepts and history, records of the Magi's appearances in magical operations are presented and analysed, with an emphasis on working components of operative sorcery from these texts. Following this, a short grammary of workings, tools, *materia*, and talismans combines modern expressions of the Magi's magic with operations and formulary from my personal practice.

This work is both an elucidation of a modern folk necromancy centred around spiritual conceptions (mainly medieval and early modern) of the mysteries and sorceries of the Magi, and an analytical survey of the historical evidence for those conceptions—especially their grimoiric and folk magical expressions. This work also encourages exploration of the iconography and mythos of the Three Kings more broadly for its ancestral-necromantic value and meaning. This manuscript is, at its core, a collection of resources for

A BOOK OF THE MAGI

honouring and working the spirits of deceased magicians—
both historically known and anonymous—across time,
space, and culture.

The Magi are important Scriptural exemplars of both
Christian and pagan knowledge, authority, and power. Even
more so than Saint Cyprian—whose crux at the crossroads
places his pagan sorcery firmly behind him—the Magi are
both enlightened and heathen, simultaneously amongst
the most elite of pagan sorcerers and the very first *followers*
of the light that announces the Son of God. They exist in
flux between their authority in their own distant lands and
their obeisance at the culmination of their Adoration. Their
mythic cycle is a pilgrimage, following a new light by old
ways of reading it.

They play a role in the coming of the light of the Son,
which they perform by the light of the Star and their understanding of the meaning of the movements of the heavens.
They are cited throughout millennia of historical debates
over the theological status of astrology in particular, and
divination in general. They are the paragons of occult
virtue, held up as precedent for the pious use of augury and
even sorcery. For may we not secure the delivery of gifts by
our star-lore and timely adorations? By the lights and signs,
the foreign magician-kings did know of a coming shift in
the world, and elected to journey to the sacred heart of it.

In setting out on this journey the Magi are cast as both
solemn pious mystics seeking truth and as savvy divin-
ers inspecting the heavens and acting accordingly and
opportunely. They are literally magicians conducting an
important ritual, political as well as cosmological. These
allegorical alchemists wander through the wilds of darkness
and the deserts of dross for an audience with the broken wa-

ters of life under a starry lamp of enlightenment. They are patrons and protectors of sacred life journeys, of plotting and navigating transitions, of summoning the endurance to continue on through unknown terrain.

They represent a cited ideal held aloft by preceding and deceased generations of (Christian) magicians, occultists, and mystics. As such, we might consider their icon a potent locus about which we might cohere ancestors—whether blood, lineage, or simply inspirational—who were magical practitioners. Devotion becomes a bridge, a common Star by which we journey. We too honour and celebrate their mysteries, their magic, and their meanings. We come together in Epiphany.

Considering the diverse lands and cultures the Magi are said to travel from, they might also be celebrated as those who convoke disparate or even somewhat eclectic practices into a common goal, journey, and work. The universalism of folk catholicism, considered as worldview rather than doctrine, is once more given a means to behold and engage with a world of many wonders. Likewise, Protestant and other post-Reformation approaches to Biblical agents are pertinent. Moreover, in bringing together different perspectives into a common conjunction, the banner of the Magi can illustrate, embody, and celebrate epistemological and pedagogical processes useful for working in developing direct spirit tutorship.

While the Magi demonstrate to an extent a certain acknowledged validity of pre-Christian knowledge and magic, that validity is founded around the crux of their ultimate acquiescence to the greater king. Matthew tells us they arrive asking for 'the king of the Jews', although as we shall see, later Christian chronicles and exegesis often imply their

A BOOK OF THE MAGI

prophecy extends to knowledge of His divine status. Other than associations with kings in prophecy, evidence for the exact power and majesty of the Magi is a little unclear. Certainly their journey to bestow their gifts of tribute upon the Nazarene is their most noble and significant act, at least in the scant Scriptural account of their footsteps.

Working with those dead magicians that come forth to honour the Magi includes not simply devotees, but also emulators of these mythic figures. Some of these spirits can be conceived of as mirroring the Magi's works of coming when summoned and bringing gifts. Some of these generous spirits' most important gifts can be tutelage offered to the practitioner: the Magi's epiphany. This comprehension of the Magi and their legions can itself inform their conjuration, whereby one can emphasise willingness in sharing the wealth of their knowledge and power.

Ultimately, emulation of generosity emerges from piety. The Magi are Wise Men not simply because they follow the Star, but because they pay homage to the King of Kings. All knees must bend. Making devotion to the Magi presents Mysteries concerning adoration and submission. Yet it also presents more practical sorcerous workings, workings of perseverance, and of domination. The Magi and their retinues can serve with both hands.

PART I:

The Cult of the Magi

The Day of Epiphany

The origins of Epiphany, the Feast of the Kings, may be older than we expect.

The early Christian feast may have descended from a pre-Christian celebration in Egypt on the evening of 5 January that commemorated the sun god Aion's birth to a virgin. This feast featured the blessing of the Nile, whose water was said to turn to wine. Our first record of the Christian feast of the epiphany occurs among eastern Christians of the early second century, who celebrated on that night and (perhaps with something of a hangover) on the following morning of 6 January.[1]

---

1 Richard C. Trexler, *The Journey of the Magi: Meanings in History of a Christian Story* (Princeton: Princeton UP, 1997), 9. See also F. Kampers, 'Der Kosmokrator in einem altfranzösischen Märchen', *Historisches Jahrbuch* 47 (1927): 467 seq.

A BOOK OF THE MAGI

Thus begins Richard C. Trexler's book on the art history of the Magi's impact and meaning, an excellent text we will be referring to throughout this more explicitly magical exploration which you now hold in your hands. As we shall see, Epiphany is tied to a number of rites and festivities concerning water and drinking.

Chiefly however is the importance—and specifically Christian importance—of 6th January as a proposed original birthday of the Saviour.[2] Not until after the cultural tectonic shift of mass conversions following Constantine's Edict of Milan—which decriminalised Christianity in 313 CE—was the Mass of Christ celebrated on our more familiar 25th December, specifically from 354 CE.[3] Neither is this the only christological significance to this date: 'from the second century the eastern churches had celebrated the baptism of Christ, by John the Baptist, on 6 January', by its Greek name Epiphany by the fourth century in Gaul.[4] Some Christians, appropriately in the east, 'chose that date to recall John's baptism of Jesus in the Jordan'; likewise, 'the marriage banquet at Cana, at which Jesus turned water into wine, and Jesus' multiplication of the loaves and fishes' were similarly celebrated or considered to have occurred on this day; and finally, as Trexler points out, 'to these narrative evocations of the early Egyptian celebration may be added a ritual one: on 6 January eastern Christians baptized newcomers and blessed holy water'.[5]

One more ancient precursor to Epiphany includes a rit-

2 K. Holl, 'Der Ursprung des Epiphanienfestes', *Sitzungsberichte der königlich preussichen Akademie der Wissenschaften* 29 (1917): 403f.
3 H. Kehrer, *Die Heiligen Drei Könige in Literatur and Kunst* (Hildesheim, 1976), 1:25f.
4 Ronald Hutton, *Stations of the Sun: A History of the Ritual Year in Britain* (Oxford: Oxford UP, 2001), 3.
5 Trexler, 9.

THE CULT OF THE MAGI

ual demonstrating a nexus of authority and water mysteries. The Byzantine 'feast of lights' was celebrated on January 6th, at which it was customary for the emperor to promote someone to the high office of *magistros*. At this event, the blessing of the water was considered 'the ecclesiastic highlight of the eastern feast of the epiphany', as:

> in the presence of other officials, the emperor and the patriarch thrice drank that blessed water around a sacred table. In contemporary toasts elsewhere in Europe we find the corollary, and in the future Epiphany cry, 'Le roi boît!' ['The king drinks!'] we may find the evocation of such Byzantine toasts.[6]

Thus, we may begin to see more clearly the manners in which celebrating the Magi parallel saint venerations, such as the toasting of saints ('Bibe amorem S. Ioannes!' ['drink the love of Saint John']).[7] In light of these likely roots in a ceremony of empowerment through blessed waters it is also especially pertinent to note the Epiphany custom of consecrating dedicated sacred water, *Dreikonigswasser*, which Joseph H. Peterson translates as 'triple-kings water' and describes as 'simply holy water blessed during the feast of the Three Kings on January 6... People would sprinkle it on doorways and around the house to bless it'.[8]

---

6 Ibid., 47.

7 Trexler, 221; Ekkehardi IV, `Casus S. Galli', in *Monumenta Germaniae Historia, Scriptores* (Hannover, 1829), 2:84. The love in the phrase is not necessarily the love for John, but John's love of God. As one German herbal medical treatise would later put it, `drink the love of Joannis, learn to love God, as *John* loved, and taught to love'. Joannes Baptista Josephus Greitter, *Nutzbares Kräuter-Büschelein für Gesunde und Krancke in fremden Gärten* (1754), 559. The present author's translation.

8 Joseph H. Peterson, *Sixth and Seventh Books of Moses* (Lake Worth: Ibis Press,

The Coming of
the Kings

¶Funerary Roots
The first record of the Magi being called 'the three kings'
can be found in the notes left by Abbot Caesarius of Arles
(d. 542).[9] Previously to this however, there was a rich tradition of the magi present in early Christian funerary art.
They were depicted in catacombs and on sarcophaguses
as carrying their typical gifts of gold, frankincense, and
myrrh—especially gold—as well as food and other fine offerings. Significantly, these were not mere decoration, but held
soteriological (if not necromantic) significance:

> Some sarcophaguses actually show the deceased in their
> togas as part of the magi's train, at times armed with
> their own gifts, 'as if they too want to approach [the
> child] to adore him'... What they want is salvation. They
> hope to obtain it by imitating the magi, as preachers
> like Ambrose and Augustine told them to do.[10]

The notion of powerful mythic figures leading a procession of attendant subordinate spirits, who may even appear
in imitation of their leader, is a familiar theme in several
traditions of spirit-lore and conjuration through Europe,
and should not be lost on us in examining these early roots

2008), 297.
9 Kehrer, *Heiligen Drei Könige*, 1:36.
10 Trexler, 24–25, quoting G. Wilpert, *I Sarcofagi Christiani Antichi* (Rome, 1929-36),
Text 2:285.

THE CULT OF THE MAGI

of our Three Kings from a practicable magical perspective. Moreover, this theme of mimicking the magi and their journey and adoration is a consistent element throughout their history and their cultic practices, and one founded on particular personal-eschatological endeavours.

We can develop these ideas of the magi and their trains of legions, as well as of spirits and their subordinates, by examining developing notions of their kingship. Trexler considers that 'as of the year 1000, the magi, now increasingly crowned in the West, might be thought of as subsidiary royalty subordinate to the *basileus* or *augustus* of different realms', and that 'this was certainly in keeping with the old concept of the magi as legates'.[11] This notion of subsidiary and subordinate royal figures certainly seems relevant to navigating the infernal hierarchies of European spiritwork traditions attested in surviving grimoiric material, and I would certainly recommend any prospective grimoirists to examine the context of such early medieval concepts of authority and emissary in closer detail.

¶How To Kneel

In more direct instances of mimicry, and indeed of our three kings acting as tutelary spirits, the magi are certainly deployed pedagogically in demonstrating how to pray. This tuition located a particularly embodied praxis, beginning with 'a type of prostration called "proskynesis"...the devotional position assumed by many a "first king" among the magi adoring Jesus in medieval art, the second being close to, and the third king usually still far from assuming that

11 Trexler, 57.

prostrate position'.[12] This kind of posture can be observed in the statuary of the Magi used to this day in crèche nativity scenes and *precepes*. More to the point, as Trexler tracks, 'with the help of a sermon from about 1130 we can demonstrate that some curate used the adoration of the magi in such plays, and consequently artistic representations of the same theme, to teach proper devotion before the divinities'.[13] The kings were mimicked through engaging with an explicit pedagogy of piety.

Just as the deceased could be depicted mirroring the Magi in presenting their gifts of devotion to the Almighty Incarnate on earth, so too their very postures could present mysteries. The Magi are approached not simply as a good example of Christian piety one could ask to put in a good word in the ear of the Divine, as in official Church doctrine of sanctioned saint devotion. Nor are they even asked for their direct assistance or worldly intercession, as in folk catholic praxes. Rather, they are the first to adore, anticipators of Christian magic and mysticism. To put it bluntly, they are ancestors more than they are heroes. As Trexler elegantly puts it, even as 'the indications of collective cult remain, however, quite slim... it is fair to say that in general, the faithful at the end of the eleventh century were more likely to pray like the magi than to them'.[14] But just how 'slim' were these cultic venerations? And, if saintly not as exactly saints, how should they be approached?

---

12 Furthermore, 'by mid-twelfth century, incidentally, paintings and sculptures, but never plays, almost uniformly show the oldest king as first in line and the youngest last in order'. Trexler, 69.

13 Trexler, 69.

14 Ibid., 73.

THE CULT OF THE MAGI

¶We Three Kings
The Magi-become-Kings are named Caspar, Balthazar, and Melchior in the fifth century, although these were not widely used until the tenth century. In the influential writings of 'Pseudo-Bede', we find some sense of individuation: Caspar as the youngest, and often a beardless youth; Balthazar as middle aged and bearded, with early indicators of being in some way 'dark' which prefigure his eventual 'Africanisation';[15] and Melchior as the eldest, an old man with long often white beard.[16] Various attributions of which King holds which gift have occurred throughout their art history, although by the early modern period the arrangement most apparently somewhat typical was Balthazar bringing gold, Melchior bringing frankincense, and Caspar bringing myrrh.

However much we may seek to differentiate and individualise the magi, as Trexler repeatedly points out, 'the truth was that none of the three had any individual identity'.[17] For instance, by around the end of the 11th century,

> the magi, no mean travellers or pilgrims themselves, emerge as the titulary saints of inns. In all these roles the magi reveal an almost invariable characteristic

15 'From the mid-thirteenth century, an occasional black servant can be found in a journey or adoration, ministering to a white king. But not until the 1360s, and then in earnest only from about 1440 onward, does the black king become common in European art'. Trexler, 102.
16 Trexler, 39; *Patrologia cursus completus... Series latina*, ed. J.-P. Migne, (Paris, 1844–64), 94:541. See also R. McNally, 'The Three Holy Kings in Early Irish Latin Writing', in *Kyriakon: Festschrift Johannes Quasten*, eds. P. Granfield and J. Jungmann, (Münster/Westf., 1970), 2:669f.
17 Trexler, 38.

23

A BOOK OF THE MAGI

of their cult in the future. The magi have power and
personality only as a collectivity and almost never as
individuals. They were not recognized as saints. There
was no significant cult to Balthasar, to Melchior, or to
Caspar.[18]

So while we may not find shrines or pilgrimage routes dedicated to any *individual* Magi,[19] we find they have a patronage by the magi (as a threesome) of inns, and by extension
travellers and pilgrims themselves. This patronage of pubs
can be observed in the sheer quantity of public houses
named the Three Kings, some in England dating back to at
least the fifteenth century.[20] Theirs is a somewhat unique
form of 'not-quite-sainthood': the magi do not officially
martyr themselves or spread the word of the Lord in a typical fashion, but they are amongst the first Gentiles to adore
the infant Nazarene, and foundational to broader tellings of
His general coming and His specific feast.

By the modern day, it should be noted, many denomina-
tions of Christianity have no problem referring to them as
saints: and it is not uncommon to see some church account
claiming this has been the case since the seventh century.
Certainly, the Catholic Encyclopedia cites a treatise, *Opus
imperfectum in Matthæum* (dated to no later than the sixth
century) contained in the writings of St. Chrysostom
which details their martyrdoms: on the 1st, 6th and 11th of

18 Ibid., 73.
19 There may be a case to be made for the coherence of a 'Saint Caspar'. His kingdom
is occasionally identified as located in the region of Egrisilla in modern day eastern
shore of the Gulf of Thailand for instance.
20 For a list of a few of these old English pubs, see Hugh Mountney, *The Three Holy
Kings of Cologne: How They Journeyed from Persia to Cologne and Their Veneration
in England* (Leominster: Gracewing, 2003), 10-11.

THE CULT OF THE MAGI

January, although accounts between this and other martyrologies differ as whether Caspar or Melchior's martyrdom occurred on the first or the second of these dates.[21] Moreover, even the author of the *Opus* apparently 'admits that he is drawing upon the apocryphal Book of Seth, and writes much about the Magi that is clearly legendary'.[22] It is certainly not my intention to claim the Three Holy Kings cannot be thought of as saints, merely to emphasise that they are at the very least a different sort of saint.

The Magi's triplicity (a term with considerable astrological significance itself) forms a basis for a variety of approaches to their religious (and magical) meaning. The Venerable Bede developed Augustinian ideas by claiming 'mystically, the three magi signify the three parts of the world, Asia, Africa, Europe'.[23] Bede furthered this conception by presenting that 'the magi could also signify the three sons of Noah, who were the fathers of these continent's races (*humanum genus*)'.[24] Thus began a long tradition of the Magi collectively representing 'all peoples of the Earth', precisely through their perceived ethnic and geographic diversity. The specific allotted racial and cultural heritages of individual magi would change over time and in different regions to serve different political and cultural agendas and reactions. This idea of the inherent foreignness of the magi provided missionaries in the so-called 'New World' a means to bring heathens into the Christian

21 Walter Drum, 'Magi', in *The Catholic Encyclopedia*, Vol. 9, (New York: Robert Appleton Company, 1910).
22 http://www.hymnsandcarolsofchristmas.com/Text/concerning_the_magi_and_their_na.htm#Note1a, last accessed 30 December 2017.
23 Trexler, 38.
24 Ibid.

A BOOK OF THE MAGI

fold (claiming—through various notions of pre-conquest evangelisation—at least one indigenous magi-king had bowed to the Messiah). Crucially, it also provided colonised early modern peoples a powerful locus about which self-determination and dissent could be fomented. Such colonisation, as we shall explore, can be considered as much an enforced submission to Christian observance than a conversion to Christian faith.

But we get a little ahead of ourselves.

||||||||||||||||||||||||||||||||||||||||||||||||||||||||||||||||||||||||||||||||||||||||||||

The Three Holy Kings of Cologne

If there it can be said to be a specifically located cult of the Three Kings, it is cohered in the bones brought to Cologne. In her travelogue-cum-material/economic history, *Travelling the Incense Route*, Barbara Toy traces the beginnings of the Wise Men's journey from the Yemeni town of Azzan, adding that 'it was around here also it is believed, that three hundred years later the emissaries of the Empress Helena came searching for "Sessania Adrumatorum"... They found the bones of the Magi and took them to Constantinople where they stayed until later taken to Milan, and finally in the twelfth century to Cologne'.[25] Specifically, the relics were 'translated to the church of St Eustorgius in Milan in the fourth century..."rediscovered" during the siege

25 Barbara Toy, *Travelling the Incense Route: From Arabia to the Levant in the Footsteps of the Magi* (London: I. B. Tauris, 2009), 19.

26

THE CULT OF THE MAGI

of Milan by the emperor Frederick Barbarossa and then translated to the cathedral of St Peter in Cologne in 1164 by Rainald von Dassel, archbishop of Cologne'.[26] The *Golden Legend*—the most important hagiographic documents of the Middle Ages[27]—repeats a version of this posthumous journey adding that since the move to Cologne, 'there they are honored by the people with great veneration and devotion'.[28] By the mid-thirteenth century, Cologne was regarded (certainly by the Inquisition of Langudoc) as one of the four major pilgrimages in Europe, along with Rome, Santiago, and Canterbury.[29]

Three bodies were indeed brought to Cologne in 1164, and while initially kept in the older cathedral of Saint Peter, they eventually found their way to their current site in 1322: 'by this time, the magi were known throughout Europe simply as "the Three Kings of Cologne"'.[30] Before the bones were installed and hallowed however, there was their gold. It was claimed in the twelfth century that the cathedral of Reims had, until the last decade of the eleventh century, owned a chalice wrought from part of the gold 'that the three magi had offered to the lord'.[31] From this point on, it

26 Eila Williamson, 160; see also Sylvia C. Harris, 'The *Historia Trium Regnum* and the Mediaeval Legend of the Magi in Germany', *Medium Aevum* 28 (1959): 23-30, here 23-24.

27 The importance of the *Golden Legend* is difficult to overstate. Famously, more copies of it were printed than the Bible. Indeed Eamon Duffy, in his introduction to the Ryan translation, dubs it 'one of the most influential books of the later Middle Ages'. Jacobus de Voragine, *The Golden Legend. Readings on the Saints*, trans. William Granger Ryan, 2 vols., (Princeton, 1993), xi.

28 *Golden Legend*, 1:84.

29 Jonathan Sumption, *Pilgrimage* (London, 1975), 104; Diana Webb, *Pilgrims and Pilgrimage in the Medieval West* (New York: I. B. Tauris, 1999), 51.

30 Trexler, 78.

31 Ibid., 72.

A BOOK OF THE MAGI

seems such claims were not infrequently made, and various treasures identified as the gold of the Magi—in the forms of objects or coins—became relics in a host of European churches.[32]

¶Gold
This gold not only presaged the cohering of a formal cultic centre in Cologne, it also came to be regarded as an expression of a deeper and incorruptible timelessness of ancient wisdom, of which the Magi were themselves merely stewards, just as these medieval churches and their reliquaries could now claim to be. In short, the gold of the Magi was the gold of Eden:

> ...referred to in the fifth- or sixth-century *Opus Imperfectum*, this lost book of the East says that the three gifts of the magi came from a treasure cavern that had been filled by Adam himself from the wealth of paradise. The magi's gold especially was thus prelapsarian in origin and had to be understood within a cosmic historical context. Coming from paradise, over the centuries it too was made to reappear at many world historical moments. Abraham had had it. Alexander the Great had possessed the gold before the magi gave it to the infant...some medieval and modern churches claimed that their chalices were made from the same gold.[33]

This link to Alexander the Great is especially interesting in light of the parallels that exist between the Magi's

32 Ibid.
33 Ibid., 39.

THE CULT OF THE MAGI

story and the history of the Macedonian's conquests of the Babylonians, who are said to have greeted him (with frankincense and other riches no less) as fulfilling an astrologically derived prophecy. Indeed, Mathieu Ossendrijver has remarked that the 'similarity to accounts of Alexander the Great's interactions with Chaldean astrologers suggests the possibility of a dependence'.[34] Ossendrijver even concludes that 'Matthew's magi most likely denote Babylonian astrologers'.[35] This is especially politically significant, as the Babylonians are the last captors of the Jewish peoples. The obeisant kneeling of these former masters before the King of the Jews has certainly been meaningful within various comprehensions of the Magi's Adoration, especially those of colonised peoples.

As a note of historicity, and to shift from considering the gold's mythic roots to its early material expression in art, we see from the early third century that 'Clement of Alexandria (d. ca. 215) had already imagined that the magi brought the golden wreaths common to Roman imperial representations, so it is not surprising that such wreaths, when not gold coins, appear on the plates with impressive frequency'.[36] Further highlighting this connection between wreaths and crowns, by the early fifth century, Orosius notes that Octavian's triple triumph had been staged on Epiphany and had been inspired by the emperor's vision

34 Mathieu Ossendrijver, 'The Story of the Magi in the Light of Alexander the Great's Encounters with the Chaldeans', in *The Star of Bethlehem and the Magi: Interdisciplinary Perspectives from Experts on the Ancient Near East, the Greco-Roman World, and Modern Astronomy*, ed. by Peter Barthel and George van Kooten (Leiden: Brill, 2015), 217.

35 Ossendrijver, 227.

36 Trexler, 23; Kehrer, *Heiligen Drei Könige*, 2:17.

29

A BOOK OF THE MAGI

of a halo around the sun.[37] The heraldry of the Magi—its crowns and coronas, along with its coins and cups—is joined by halos and wreaths.

¶The Magica Materia of the Magi
The Three Kings, as patrons of travellers and pilgrims, are a popular image included on pilgrim badges. A practice of stamping their likeness on hastily constructed clay tablets as eulogia tokens has been documented from at least the sixth century. Two particular examples of magian *eulogiae* are described by L. Y. Rahmani:

A. (Pl. 8:B). A round token, made of blackish-gray, poorly-fired clay; diameter: 2.4 cm.; maximum thickness: 0.9 cm. The reverse is concave, as if the fresh clay had been pressed by thumb onto the stamp which carried the image's negative. The relief shows, on the left, the Virgin with nimbus, sitting on a high-backed chair. On her outstretched arms, she holds the Child, a cruciform nimbus on his head; he faces forward and his left hand is raised. The three bearded Magi approach from the right bearing gifts. All wear short tunics and Phrygian caps; their legs are slightly bent at the knees. Below the Child's legs there appears a quatrefoil. The top of the token, where a star would be expected, is broken.

B. (Pl. 8:C). Similar in form, material and firing to Token A; diameter: 1.9 cm.; maximum thickness: 0.8 cm. Reverse uneven. At the left side of the relief, the Virgin with nimbus sits on a high-backed chair, holding on her

---

37 Trexler, 28; 'Dominici sacramenti', *Patrologia cursus completus*, 31:105.

THE CULT OF THE MAGI

lap the Child with nimbus. His head is in profile, facing right, and his left hand is raised. The three bearded Magi approach from the right bearing gifts; their legs are sharply bent at the knees. All three wear Phrygian caps. Above the scene a six-pointed star is shown.[38]

In giving a potted history of the practice of making and using *eulogiae*, Rahmani actually presents some fascinating inspirations and precedents for modern magical experiments. These magian images were, after all,

> devotional souvenirs fashioned in the sixth century and later at and near the Holy Places. Such *eulogiae* were made in two forms: small bottles (*ampullae*) containing either water from the sources near the Holy Places or oil from the lamps which burned at the shrines; tokens (*tortae*) made of clay or earth taken from those sites, incense prepared at the shrines, etc. All were stamped with representations of scenes from the life of Christ or of the Saints, appropriate to their place of manufacture. Although many of these *eulogiae* must have been made, few have survived. This is especially true of the tokens (*tortae*) which were intended to be used—ground into powder, dissolved in water, and swallowed for their purported miraculous properties. Thus such tokens remain scarce...[39]

38 L. Y. Rahmani, 'The Adoration of the Magi on Two Sixth-Century CE Eulogia Tokens', *Israel Exploration Journal* 29.1 (1979), 34.
39 Ibid., 34–35.

A BOOK OF THE MAGI

So these items were to be made from powerful earths, clays and dirts, from sacred sites. Far from permanent altarpieces, these tokens were made to be used as talismanic material—as much ingredient as amulet. Later operations conducted under the auspices of the Three Kings found in grimoiric records attest to the use of 'dust from the street steeped in olive oil' for works of travelling.[40] It seems pertinent to note that such a prescription, in combining the two forms of *eulogiae* mentioned above, is magically powerful and significant, even if not a matter of direct historical transmission.

From their early days to their medieval popularity, magian images demonstrate a tension between representations of the Nativity at which the Magi adored (that is, those images focusing on Mary and Child), and those which emphasised the Adoration itself and included the Virgin and Infant.[41] By the medieval period however other pilgrim badges and tokens simply depicted busts of the three magi.[42] There are some textiles that also depict the magi, although tapestry and embroidery are of course 'far less likely to survive from the medieval period'.[43] Nevertheless, we have at least one set of vestments dating from 1330–1350 depicting the Adoration of the Magi.[44] We also know 'the

40 See 'Marvelous Secrets' of 'The Black Dragon', in *Crossed Keys* (Dover: Scarlet Imprint, 2011), 59.

41 Copenhagen, Nationalmuseet, 'Pilgrim's badge of lead. Brought from Cologne. 13th century. Near Set. Kathrine Monastery in Ribe', D7744.

42 Brian Spencer, *Pilgrims Souvenirs and Secular Badges* (London, 1998), 261-66. An illustration of this badge can be found in *Gothic Art for England 1400-1547*, ed. Richard Marks and Paul Williamson (London, 2003), 426.

43 Elia Williamson, 'The Cult of the Three Kings of Cologne in Scotland', in *Saints' Cults in the Celtic World*, ed. by S. Boardman, J. Davies, and Eila Williamson (Woodbridge: Boydell, 2008), 171.

44 Bonnie Young, 'Opus Anglicanum', *The Metropolitan Museum of Art Bulletin*, new series 29 (1971): 291-98.

THE CULT OF THE MAGI

Three Kings was a popular subject of tapestry, being found in the collections of the dukes of Burgundy and English kings'.[45]

Williamson draws attention to murkily-recalled traditions of magian drinking horns—objects inscribed with the names of the kings and sometimes even a charm (*'iaspar fert miram tus melchior'*)[46]—which 'were used in the ceremonial drinking rituals of guilds and societies'.[47] Examples of such objects can be found in the Nationalmuseet in Copenhagen,[48] as well as in Bergen and Arendel.[49] Shades of the older drinking traditions of January 6th discussed earlier seem relevant to resurrect.

¶Offering The Gifts

Unsurprisingly, the most popular and arguably important magian *materia* are the gifts of gold, frankincense, and myrrh. De Voragine's *Golden Legend* presents several interpretations of the triplicity symbolism of the Gifts of the Magi. Quoting Bernard, we begin with the Gifts' relations to very practical concerns: 'they offered gold to the holy Virgin to relieve her poverty, frankincense to dispel the bad odours of the stable, and myrrh to strengthen the child's

45 Williamson, 171; citing W. G. Thompson, *A History of Tapestry. From the Earliest Times to the Present Day* (London, 1906), 77, 126, 165, 170, 263, 265, 273.
46 This is quoted and rendered into English verse in Reginald Scot's *Discovery of Witchcraft* as: 'Gasper with his myrrh began / These presents to unfold, / Then Melchior brought in Frankincense, / And Balthasar brought in Gold'. Reginald Scot, *Discovery of Witchcraft* (London, 1584: 1665 edition), 130-31. See also below in Works of Protection.
47 Williamson, 166-67.
48 Copenhagen, Nationalmusset, drinking horns with gilded bronze mounts, 10543, 382; drinking horn with gilded bronze mount, MDLXXIV.
49 George F. Black, 'Scottish Charms and Amulets', *Proceedings of the Society of Antiquaries of Scotland* 27 (1892-93): 485-86.

A BOOK OF THE MAGI

limbs and drive out harmful worms'. The trinity of Gifts
is mostly considered in light of the figure of the Nazarene
Himself. So, 'the gold was offered for tribute, the incense for
sacrifice, and the myrrh for burial of the dead... three gifts
corresponded to Christ's royal power, divine majesty, and
human mortality'. Like the Adoration of the Magi itself,
the Gifts could be taken as tutelary directives, as exemplary
actions of piety and wisdom, so: 'gold symbolizes love, incense prayer, and myrrh the mortification of the flesh; and
these three we ought to offer to Christ'. Finally, 'the gifts
signify three attributes of Christ, namely, his most precious
divinity, his most devout soul, and his intact and uncorrupt-
ed flesh'.[50] These are not the only interpretations by far, and
the practice of finding new symbolic triplicities by which to
understand the coming of the Christ Child is practically a
magian tradition in itself.

Later Renaissance interpretation by Marsilio Ficino
would emphasise a rather more occult reading, as Ficino

> points out the astrological as well as the theological
> appropriateness of the gifts the Magi brought and also
> urges the appropriateness of Gabriel's stellar disguise.
> Gold, a solar substance, bears witness to Christ's king-
> ship; [frank]incense, belonging to Venus, betokens his
> divine grace and his priesthood; myrrh, sharing in the
> jovian life that knows no decay, indicates his immortal
> Godhead. Beyond this, the gifts reveal other divine
> mysteries: for the gold was given to help a poor child;
> myrrh to strengthen the weak body of a young child;

50 *Golden Legend*, 1:83.

THE CULT OF THE MAGI

and incense perfumed the humble stable in which Christ was born.[51]

Such Ficinian analysis was very influential (as we will discuss below) and can be seen in the works of Phillipe du Mornay, who seems to extend astrological characterisation of the meeting of these Benefics as a sort of triplanetary signature of the Magi at their rendezvous: 'Here the Astrologers had matter whereupon to exercyse their Contemplations. For this Starre appeared in December, when the Sunne was in Sagittarius, in which signe (they say) both Jupiter, the Sunne, and Venus were met altogether; al which three (by their principles) betoken a most ryghtuouse, a most myghtie, and a most mercifull King, but yet poore'.[52] This tension between the Infant's humble oh-so-human birth conditions and His divine splendour as the Son of God will later become a consistent Christological mystery of course, but is perhaps especially apparent in the framing of kings bowing and adoring a poor child: a child, we should remember, that the Magi are not necessarily aware is the Son of God. It is the explicitly the majesty rather than the divinity of the Christ-child that is honoured in the devotions of the Three Kings.

There was—very understandably, if not terribly imaginatively—a tradition of English kings offering the Gifts of gold, frankincense, and myrrh back to the Three Kings; a tradition best known as being enacted by Edward III,

51 Stephen M. Buhler, 'Marsilio Ficino's *De stella magorum* and Renaissance Views of the Magi', *Renaissance Quarterly* 43.2 (Summer, 1990): 356–57.
52 Philippe de Mornay, *A Woorke concerning the trewnesse of the Christian Religion* (London, 1587), 631.

A BOOK OF THE MAGI

Richard II, and Henry VII.[53] Likewise, we know James IV seems to have fairly regularly offered three French crowns (equivalent to 42 shillings) on Epiphany.[54] This offering of 'crowns' can perhaps be contextualised in light of a practice that seems to have been popularised by a vision received by the famed mystic Elizabeth of Shonau, who died on 18 June 1164: the year the relics of the magi arrived in Cologne. Elizabeth's vision had two pertinent details: firstly, she saw 'the three kings first taking off their crowns and offering them to Jesus, who takes them and then returns them to the monarchs',[55] and secondly, 'the first king gave Jesus a large gold coin that seemed to bear a royal image'.[56] Eventually, the symbolic offering as well as real tithing of regal headgear and precious coinage alike would be regular features of magian procession, mystery plays, and Epiphany practices. Such a custom may also be familiar to astute necromancers as informing the instructions of *De Nigromancia* to offer the book's patron, Saint Cyprian, a crown upon 'his book' in preparation for carrying out the operations contained therein...[57]

There is also evidence of at least one monarch stipulating the funding of pilgrimages. Queen Margaret I of Denmark 'in her will of 1410, had provided payment for a

---

53 Shelagh Mitchell, 'Richard II: Kingship and the Cult of the Saints', in *The Regal Image of Richard II and the Wilton Diptych*, ed. Dillian Gordon, Lisa Monnas and Caroline M. Barron (London: Harvey Miller, 1997), 123; Hutton, *Stations of the Sun*, 16.
54 Williamson, 172; citing *Treasurer's Accounts*, II.268, III.285, IV.181.
55 Trexler, 70.
56 Ibid.
57 *De Nigromancia*, ed. by Michael Albion MacDonald (Gillette: Heptangle, 1988) 9. For further discussion of the Cyprianic patronage of this nigromantic manuscript, see Alexander Cummins, '"In The Manner of Saint Cyprian": A Cyprianic Black Magic of Early Modern English Grimoires', in *Cypriana: Old World*, ed. Alexander Cummins, Jesse Hathaway Diaz, and Jennifer Zahrt (Seattle: Revelore Press, 2017), 83-116.

THE CULT OF THE MAGI

number of men to go on various pilgrimages on her behalf', which of course 'included three men to go to the Three Holy Kings in Cologne'.[58] This notion of funding others to pilgrimage-by-proxy as a posthumous act seems to once more hearken back, if only poetically, to the sarcophaguses of the earliest depictions of the magi: the dead queen symbolically following the Three Wise Men. It also perhaps suggests a devotional modality to modern practitioners and devotees in this age of crowd-funded pilgrimages and expeditions.

Finally, in her essay on their cultus in Scotland, Williamson concludes 'Scottish dedications to the Three Kings of Cologne all relate to altars and date to either the end of the fifteenth century or early sixteenth century'.[59] Other saints would frequently be honoured at these altars—especially Masses dedicated to those saints such as Anne and Joseph who were part of the actual Holy Family. As such, enterprising magicians might consider etching the names of the Three Kings into their altars themselves, instead of (or as well as!) potentially investing in some Nativity statuary.

¶Magian Charms

As with the workings pulled from the grimoiric record we will explore in depth later in this book, the inscription upon rings and other sacred jewellery of 'the names of the Three Kings were used as charms against epilepsy, headache, fevers, the dangers of travel, sudden death and sorcery'.[60] 'Cramp rings' were issued on Good Friday by English

58 Williamson, 174; Webb, 141–42.
59 Williamson, 177.
60 Ibid., 167.

37

A BOOK OF THE MAGI

monarchy from the fourteenth century up to the time of the Tudors, and a fifteenth-century medical treatise instructed them to bear the three names inscribed on the inside of the rings.[61]

There are many examples in the material history records of fourteenth and fifteenth-century amuletic items bearing the names of the Three Kings.[62] As already discussed, the magi graced various pilgrim badges, which, while sacred, might not have been considered exactly 'talismanic'. To this, Brian Spencer specifically notes that a ca. 1360 brooch found in London (engraved with 'CASPER MELCHIOR BPTIS') to be far more likely to be an amulet than a pilgrimage souvenir.[63]

IIIIIIIIIIIIIIIIIIIIIIIIIIIIIIIIIIIIIIIIIIIIIIIIIIIIIIIIIIIIIIIIIIIIIIIIIIIIIIIIIIIIIIIIIIIIIIIII

Star Singers

If such amulets represent a more magical side to magian material history, then certainly astrology—especially that of emergent Italian city-states of the late medieval and early modern ages—emphasised the occult dimensions of the Magi's power and wisdom in their intellectual history:

---

61 Ronald Hutton, *Stations of the Sun*, 188; cited in Williamson, 167.

62 See for instance Mary B. Deery, *Medieval Ring Brooches in Ireland: A Study of Jewellry, Dress and Society* (Wicklow: Bray, Co., 1998), 72, 109–10; Black 'Scottish Charms and Amulets', 486, 487; Ellen Ettlinger, 'British Amulets in London Museums', *Folklore* 50 (1939), 167, 168; *Gothic Art for England* 333, fn. 211; D. H. Caldwell, *Angels, Nobles and Unicorns: Art and Patronage in Medieval Scotland* (Edinburgh, 1982), 90 (E71); J. Graham Callander, 'Fourteenth-century Brooches and other Ornaments in the National Museum of Antiquities of Scotland', *Proceedings of the Society of Antiquaries of Scotland* 58 (1923/24), 183–84.

63 Spencer, *Pilgrimage Souvenirs*, 264, fn. 98.

THE CULT OF THE MAGI

specifically and especially 'Italian intellectuals showed much interest in the star and the intellectual caste of the magi that had watched the heavens'.[64] In terms of their treatment by Renaissance occult philosophers and magical practitioners, Ficino references the Magi frequently[65] and Stephen M. Buhler concludes 'Ficino's enthusiasm for the Magi—and for the ancient theology they were thought to have inherited—proved contagious for several generations'.[66] Of particular note is a sermon written by Ficino, *De stella magorum*, which 'helped to shape the perception and treatment of the Magi not only in the Neoplatonic tradition but in broader Christian and literary traditions as well'.[67] Specifically, 'the *De stella*, along with some of Ficino's other observations on the Magi, was widely known throughout the sixteenth and seventeenth centuries and was frequently cited'.[68] Buhler identifies two important aspects of Ficino's Magi. Firstly, they are mediators between pagan and Jewish-and-eventually-Christian knowledge, even wisdom, meaning we should study their occult doctrines and practices; and secondly, these practices were definitely astrological, legitimating the starry craft.

Of these first points—that the Magi can hold lineage claims wider than the Jewish Patriarchs—we must understand the idea of uncovering God's original perfect transmission in antiquity: the notion of the *prisca theologia*. As Buhler relates:

64 Trexler, 122.
65 Buhler, 348.
66 Ibid., 370.
67 Ibid., 348.
68 Ibid., 351.

A BOOK OF THE MAGI

In Ficino's presentation, the Magi are active participants within the *prisca theologia*... The Magi are, therefore, worthy inheritors, as well as direct recipients, of some awareness of the truly divine, as were many of the pagan philosophers and seers who preceded them. Hermes Trismegistus and Zoroaster were sometimes regarded as gentile Moses figures—or, alternatively, as students of Moses himself—and their supposed philosophic progeny, from Orpheus to Pythagoras to Plato, were accordingly compared with the Old Testament prophets.[69]

Once more, the Magi are brought back into the Christian heavenly fold, like so many approved pagan philosophers and Hebrew Patriarchs. Of the second point, we may summarise that 'the fact that God had spoken to the Magi in astrological terms had two important consequences for Ficino: first, it was another indication that pagan learning could be a path toward faith and could provide corroboration of Christian beliefs; second, it seemed to be a divine validation of the study and practice of the pagan mysteries'.[70]

Not only did the story of the Magi validate astrology, but by Ficino's assessment, the component icons and events of the story could be interpreted astrologically. This began, naturally, with the nature, position and timing of the Star itself:

Ficino therefore speculates as to what kinds of astrological investigation might have been useful to the Magi;

69 Ibid., 348.
70 Ibid., 359.

THE CULT OF THE MAGI

he considers such factors as the colors of the comet's rays and the planetary conjunctions that provided a backdrop for the comet. Perhaps—Ficino does stress the conjectural nature of his ideas here—the Magi knew that the comet was a favorable omen because the color of its rays revealed that the comet shared in the natures of favorable planets: the Sun's gold, Jupiter's silver, and Venus' mixture of both colors. Leaden colored rays, being saturnian, or fiery red ones, being martian, would have been appropriate only for a more dire event. The Sun, Jupiter, and Venus were all probably within Sagittarius, and their positions in the heavens would have caused the Magi no little wonder and consternation, for while the presence of these planets indicated that the child would be 'most just', 'most renowned', and 'most merciful', the Sun's location in the ascendant suggested that he would not be rich. Further, while the position of Jupiter led them to conclude that the newborn king's mother would be eminently fertile, the fact that the Moon was in the first face of Virgo argued for sterility and virginity. They could not fully understand how a king could be both great and poor [though, again, not necessarily understood yet as Divine], how the paradox of 'fertile sterility' could be resolved in the miracle of the Virgin Birth. Still, they were able to ascertain his true kingship from Jupiter, and that his reign would be marked by truth and grace from the Sun and Venus.[71]

Further along in his *De Stella* sermon-treatise, 'Ficino considers other astrological possibilities: the dominant sign

71 Ibid., 355.

41

A BOOK OF THE MAGI

might have been Virgo, not Sagittarius; according to the opinion of Albumasar, among others, the first decan image in Virgo, which is that of a beautiful maiden giving suck, may have served as an important sign for the Magi'.[72] Astrological timings and heraldry begin to be more fully realised and cohered as significant loci of magian cultus.

We should also note that Ficino's magian theories were not simply academic theorisation—there were also real social and political implications to his considerations of the Magi. Indeed, Ficino's magian 'fascination may have been further encouraged by his patrons' dealings with a Florentine lay-religious society, the Compagnia de' Magi', an organisation of some significant 'importance for the Medici and in Florentine life'.[73] This nexus of socio-political influence and religious meaning is especially evidenced, Buhler judges, in the 'sermonizing' of *De Stella* that 'reflects the devotional function of the group: its assemblies for prayer and adoration were meant to help its members in emulating the Magi, who were viewed as the group's patron saints'.[74] Once more, a pedagogical mimesis is foregrounded, with the Three Kings taken as sacred exemplars of wisdom and righteousness. As we shall now see, this mimicry extended into full costuming and re-enactment, further extending

---

72 'The mention of Albumasar, who had actually cast a horoscope for Christ, seems to have intensified Ficino's sense of caution and to have prompted him to make an important point about astral signification. Because one of the Church's major criticisms of astrology was its infringement upon the freedom of the divine will in the case of Christ's Nativity, Ficino must echo a venerable disclaimer. This super-celestial comet, he writes, was only a sign, a source of information having no direct causal relation to the events of the Incarnation: the comet was "non causa Christi, sed signum."' Buhler, 358–59.

73 Ibid., 350.

74 Ibid., 351.

THE CULT OF THE MAGI

the economic as well as socio-political impact of these cultic practices.

|||||||||||||||||||||||||||||||||||||||||||||||||||||||||||||||||||||||||||||||||||||||||||||||||||

Procession, Plays, Pageantry and Protest

¶Processional Lines and Lineage
As their cultus developed, the Magi began to simultaneously fill two sets of functions. Firstly, as evidenced by the narratives of them representing Three Races of Man, 'the story of the magi was assuming a position as a mythic narrative about fundamental realities: the shape of the cosmos, the classification of its peoples, the generational characteristics of humanity, the sources of wealth in that universe, natural treasure as the stuff of history, and the concept of history as a constant recirculation of significant objects'.[75] We see this object-centricity in the veneration and circulation of their gold, representing their meaningful lineage as well as their immediate wealth.

Such celebration and strengthening of lineage is especially interesting in light of both certain royal traditions of self-depiction and in the public expression of magian pageants and processions. This tradition of monarchs representing themselves as magi extended to their sons, who were often painted or embroidered on tapestries as

75 Trexler, 40.

43

A BOOK OF THE MAGI

either the youngest of the Three Kings or one of their legates. King Hans of Denmark (1481–1513) is thought to be
depicted as the eldest kneeling magi in the Adoration scene
of an altarpiece made in Antwerp around 1520, 'while the
figure to his right, who is standing, is thought to be his
son Christian II (1513–23)'.[76] This seems especially pertinent to meditations on lineage and the magi, given that
Christian was named after his grandfather. Nor was this
custom of the ages of man being represented in the Three
Kings through fathers and sons limited to private tapestry
and royal finery. In the Florentine *festa* of 1468, 'the young
members of the Confraternity of the Magi had created
such convincing masks of their fathers and had learned the
latters' gestures so perfectly that, in launching the parade
to the palace of Herod (the journey), they actually seemed
to be their fathers joining the parade'.[77] The imitating of
fathers by sons, of descendents mimicking their forefathers,
furthers the conceptions and applications of mimesis in
magian devotional practices. Here too we have a shining
instance of the Magi's *ancestral* significance and potency—
of their power and grace for honouring our forefathers and
foremothers, whether by blood, by lineage, or by tradition—
as iconography and imitational actions for magian coher-
ences of communion with dead magicians.

¶A Pageantry of Peasantry
The Wise Men also began to articulate certain 'bottom-up'
sets of social interrelations:

---

76 Williamson, 175; Poul Grinder-Hansen, *Danish Middle Ages and Renaissance*,
trans. Philip Ronald Davies, Guides to the National Museum (Copenhagen, 2002), 105.
77 Trexler also notes that this 'play so departed from normal convention that its real
focus was not the kings but their legates or youthful messengers'. Trexler, 92.

THE CULT OF THE MAGI

the three kings or magi of the Bible became part of
the festive life of Christian Europe—people began to
play the magi—in some relation to the ancient practice
of electing and crowning seasonal or festive kings, a
practice which, as we have seen in Byzantium, easily
operated separate from the story of the evangelical magi
and from an agrarian economy. After all, Jesus was, so
to speak, elected king by the magi. Even today, electing a boss or leader for a particular job or feast is as
much an urban as it is a village custom. There are social
processes. Relating such processes to a story, like that of
the magi, comes afterward.[78]

And thus peoples across Europe began to dress and en-
act as the Magi—their journey, their Adoration, and even
their very kingship—a kingship which, we should remind
ourselves, is not explicitly present in the thin Scriptural
description given by Matthew. Mimicry took on a further
context and set of utilities. Costuming the parts of the
Three Kings themselves for magian plays offered somewhat
unique opportunities for guilds to market their expertise
and wealth, and the 'decorative harnesses and saddles that
adorn the Magi's mounts in the foreground might serve a
further purpose of advertising the guild's products'.[79] Eila
Williamson agrees that 'in medieval urban plays throughout Europe it was often the goldsmiths' or the tailors' guilds
that were responsible for pageants featuring the Three
Kings of Cologne, presumably because these guilds would

78 Trexler, 53, fn 34.
79 Vida J. Hull, 'Spiritual Pilgrimage in the Paintings of Hans Memling', in *Art and Architecture of Late Medieval Pilgrimage*, ed. Sarah Blick and Rita Tekippe (Leiden: Brill, 2004), 1:35.

be able to supply the requisite precious gifts and regal clothing'; yet she also emphasises both sacred and profane considerations: 'urban drama involving guilds was also a means by the which a guild could advertise its products as well as demonstrate its integration into salvific history'.[80] There is still a soteriological significance: but we move from images of the faithful following the Magi in their Journey and Adoration on sarcophaguses, to actually instantiating the wealth and splendour of the Kings in public spectacle and ceremony.

A major set of shifts occurred in the early modern period regarding magian pageants, in which subservient giving unto a higher power was enshrined as a height of piety. The Magi began not bringing gifts but receiving tithe and begging alms: 'spatial and moral focus of Epiphany celebrations shifted from altars to crèches and from kings giving to kings begging'.[81] This provided at least two vital sets of socio-political meaning to such King-masking. Firstly, it reconfigured Epiphany as a time to collect taxes: just as the magi had given to the Christ-child, so should devout Christians give to their divinely-appointed monarch. Secondly though, across early modern Europe, 'those who played the magi were poor and begged from the rich'.[82] This second set of practices involved the poor demanding from the wealthy, under the auspices of both precedence of celebrating the Messiah, devotion to the Almighty, and *as* themselves taking on a mantle of holy kings. The radicalism that such practices could foster should not be underappreciated.

80 Williamson, 165.
81 Trexler, 159.
82 Ibid., 170.

THE CULT OF THE MAGI

¶The Night of the Kings

Such potential for politicisation and dissent in these magian rites was certainly exacerbated through the lens of colonialism in the occupied 'New World'. Trexler states that 'the period that began in the late 1530s was one of considerable unrest throughout New Spain, and it will come as little surprise to find that the figure of the magi was part of the cultural backdrop to these uprisings'.[83] This is a fascinating instance of how efforts to convert native populaces gave them mythic structures that could be adopted to challenge that very colonising authority. By notions of pre-conquest evangelisation, missionaries had framed their work as simply 'reminding' native peoples that they were already Christian and had simply forgotten. How else could the crosses and developed civilisation of the Maya people be understood? What this amounted to was not merely a colonisation of peoples or cultures, but of these cultures' histories and their dead, subsuming the achievements of their ancestors into the fold of European or European-inspired accomplishments.[84]

Such missionary work was not limited to the Americas. In every instance though, the Three Kings provided a means for the ancestors of colonised peoples to cohere and own their own significance. Beginning as a tutelary exemplar of the powerful, it nevertheless put an ancestral face on an edifice of authority:

83 Ibid., 155.
84 For more on the political and theological specifics of colonial Christendom, and especially how the linguistics of conversion can agglutinise indigenous and invading traditions to expand without eradicating or even recuperating native beliefs, customs and identities, see Vincent James Stanzione, *Rituals of Sacrifice: Walking the Face of the Earth on the Sacred Path of the Sun* (Albuquerque: University of New Mexico Press, 2003).

A BOOK OF THE MAGI

Portuguese missionaries also made use of the magi
theme in their Indian evangelization efforts...they
would use the magi to teach potential converts how to
pray, just as European clergy had long used the kings to
that same end. Suddenly, the traditionally black magus
becomes an Indian prince, demonstrating a missionary
flexibility that we shall encounter in the Americas as
well.[85]

Indigenous and colonised peoples were told that a magi-
cian-king ancestor of theirs had already paid tribute and
recognised the divinity and authority of (European versions
of) the Nazarene and his ministers and Church Militant.
Yet this very story of colonial legitimisation also proffered
a corona of a brighter dawn after a dark night. Continuing
European masking and begging traditions of the kings col-
lecting representational tribute, 'the colonial rulers of the
Americas watched apprehensively each year as the wretched
of the earth exercised their right to dress up, conceal their
identities, and then demand some greater or lesser redis-
tribution of wealth during the feast of kings'.[86] The Three
Kings going begging in the name of the Lord had already
come to 'identify themselves with the conquered'.[87] *All*
knees would indeed bow.

Smash-cut to Mexico City, 1609:

A rumor circulated regarding a rising of the blacks. It
was said that on the previous 5 January, the night of

85 Trexler, 135.
86 Ibid., 155.
87 Ibid.

THE CULT OF THE MAGI

the Kings, many blacks had joined together and elected
a king, and others with titles like dukes and counts,
and other princes found in any government. And even
though this rumor spread through the city, in the first
place it troubled the spirits of the viceroy and the other
lords of the Audiencia.[88]

The shackles placed by colonial masters upon the ancestors
of their servants and slaves had been thrust into the fire of
their nightmares and had been forged back into crowns.
Hierarchies were whispered to have been established, kings
elected and titles of nobility bestowed—devilish in the eyes
of their oppressors—whether in bloody mockery, in earnest
self-determination, or simply in remembrance of the hor-
rors faced at the blunt end of exploitation. In the hands of
the colonised, the necromancy of the Kings shook colonial
masters to their core from beneath the earth they had
claimed as their own.

||||||||||||||||||||||||||||||||||||||||||||||||||||||||||||||||||||||||||||||||||||||||

Towards a Nigromancy
of the Magi

The nigromancy of the cultus of the Three Holy Kings
begins with their images leading processions of the devout
through their own personal eschatological pilgrimages, and
extends to their relics eventually rendering Cologne a major
European pilgrimage site. These translated bones can be

88 Ibid., 156.

A BOOK OF THE MAGI

considered to have called the further developments of their cultus into being. As Trexler summarises:

> the absence of a cult or even of individual personalities does not imply an absence of social significance. Even as faceless messengers, they were important to early Christian life and society... Nameless magi stand at the beginnings of European liturgical and popular drama during period. Their gold will precede their bodies as a relic in Europe, just as their bodies preceded their names on the altars of Cologne.[89]

Aptly re-membering their sepulchral origins upon sarcophaguses and the walls of catacombs, the very bones of the Magi can be thought in this historical and mythic sense to have cohered their cultus into being. This necromantic black magic was well recognised by Luther and Calvin, who bitterly criticised the relics as fake, the cultus as a cashgrab ('*pecuniae causa*'), and urged his listeners and followers not to go on pilgrimage to further support this sham of a lie. Despite this critique, 'the Reformers' condemnations only very slowly affected the geography of central European celebrations of the Epiphany in subsequent centuries', and 'in general, the rites associated with Kings' Day that were celebrated in Catholic Europe after the reformation can be documented in Protestant Europe as well'.[90]

There is a cosmologically political dimension to this nigromancy, to this forbidden but nevertheless tasted fruit, going well beyond Restoration protest and propaganda.

89 Ibid., 45.
90 Ibid., 158.

THE CULT OF THE MAGI

The otherness of the Magi is a continual tension that both legitimates and subverts centralised authority. Just as the magi could be depicted as all the races of the world, or all the ages of man, so too are there considerations of the potential effeminacy of these foreign dignitaries with their alien expression, modes of dress and comportment, and cultural mores. As 'males like Matthew reach into space and fetch outside magi to prove their Lord is king and God, thus reaching into the future of time...with the power from outside, forecasting the future, there comes the danger of youth, the threat of women'.[91] Furthermore, posthumously further othered by colonisers and celebrated by the colonised—a theme perhaps once more highlighted by a recognition of the wise men of the Babylonian former masters offering gifts and submission—there is indeed a powerful nigromantic outsider current animating the Three Kings.

To leave you with but one further instance of this potential for so-called 'black magic', I can demonstrate a distinctly Christian folk necromancy present in even the most famous of folk rites associated with the Three Kings. I speak, of course, of the CMB formula. As Joseph H. Peterson briefly describes how, come the Feast of the Three Kings on January 6th, such folk would (and still do!), 'write "C + M + B " and the year in chalk over the doorway to protect the home. (C + M + B stands for 'Caspar, Melchior, and Balthasar' or alternately, *Christus mansionem benedicat*—'Christ bless this house').'[92]

It is thought such practices may have been popularised by the German *Sternsinger* tradition—a carolling custom

91 Ibid., 123.
92 Peterson, *Sixth and Seventh Books of Moses*, 297.

51

A BOOK OF THE MAGI

celebrating the Journey by Magian re-enactors carrying a star door-to-door and singing or reciting prayers for the protection of the residences they visited—which appears to have grown in popularity from the sixteenth century.

Contemporary practices feature splitting the four figures of the year on either side of the central motto. Thus, in the year this book will be born, you will find 2 0 +C +M +B +1 8 chalked above many a devotee's door. I have also seen versions in which the whole formula is also bracketed by extra crosses and thus rendered +2 0 +C +M +B +1 8 + or formulations where the digits are interspersed between the initials, as 2 C 0 M 1 B 8, both with and without crosses between the letter and numbers. If you engage in no other magian practice as the result of reading this book, and make no other commitment, at least allow the three names to protect the entrance to your home and bless your journeys through it into the world. Orisons to bless your chalk are provided in the later section of this book.

And yet, there is in fact a variation on this formula: ethnographers of southern German-speaking have found chalked on or above house doors 'C +M +B +E +E '.[93] What are these extra letters? There is a strong case for their representing Enoch and Elijah—two prophets sometimes considered to have been assumed bodily into heaven, undying and immortal. Their particular relationship to the Magi requires us to familiarise ourselves with the work of Jacques d'Auzoles Lapeyre, a seventeenth-century sacred-geographer who became increasingly focused on the notion that these two prophets, along with Melchizedek, were 'still alive, in body and soul, although it had been three thou-

---

93 P. Sartori, *Sitte und Brauch* (Leipzig, 1910–14), 3:77.

THE CULT OF THE MAGI

sand, seven hundred years since [they] blessed Abraham'.[94]
D'Auzoles considered that they had assumed the roles
of 'mediums for the revelation of heavenly secrets to
humanity'.[95] Crucially, he also asserted that the Three Kings
who visited the infant at Bethlehem were none other than
these three undying prophets: Gaspar was in fact Enoch,
Melchior was Melchizedek, and Balthazar was Elijah.[96] Obviously, 'd'Auzoles's imaginative speculation—some unchar-
itable souls called it lunacy—did not, to be sure, singlehand-
edly open up a whole new way of looking at the magi', yet
'like the Jewish prophets d'Auzoles now held them to be',
the magi—renowned after all for their astrological skills—
'had long been conceived as supernaturals able to help the
living determine what the heavens had in store for them'.[97]
The appeal to the Magi's example to justify contemporary
Christian astrology is a very old one, but this concept added
an extra specificity. One did not simply interpret the stars
like the Three Kings, but could do so *with* the Magi, spiritu-
ally at least.

✝ ✝ ✝

94 Jacques d'Auzoles Lapeyre, *Melchisedech, ou Discours auquel on voit qui est ce
grand Prestre-Roy...* (Paris, 1622); cited in Trexler, 188.
95 *The Encyclopedia of Religions*, ed. M. Eliade (New York, 1987), 5:93.
96 Jacques d'Auzoles Lapeyre, *L'Epiphanie, ou Pensées nouvelles à la Gloire de Dieu
touchant les trois Mages* (Paris, 1638) 243ff. Quoted in Trexler, 188.
97 Trexler, 188.

PART II:
||||||||||||||

The Works of the Three Holy Kings

||||||||||||||||||||||||||||||||||||||||||||||||||||||||||||||||||||||||||||||||||||||||||||||

The Cakes of the Kings

Epiphany, the Feast of the Three Kings, El Día De Los Reyes, Dreikönigstag, Los Tres Reyes, and Twelfth Night are, of course, still celebrated to this day around the world. Especially outside the Anglo-sphere, these are often public occasions of great spectacle and celebration. Floats and processions are made and displayed. In many countries, particularly in Latin America, it is the day that children receive their gifts, trumping Christmas Day. Other traditions observed in France and even Cuba include placing one's shoes at the threshold of one's bedroom or house on the night of January 5th—children often wake in the morning to discover them filled with sweets or other presents, presenting a parallel to Anglo-American customs of hanging stockings, as well as a further chance for meditation on the magian mysteries of sacred travelling. In many parts of the world, children leave presents out for the Three Kings, as other children do for Father Christmas or Santa Claus and

54

THE WORKS OF THE THREE HOLY KINGS

his reindeer: a plate of biscuits, water, and of course grass
or hay for their camels. I have even had it related to me in
personal correspondence that there exist traditional beliefs
concerning the Three King's camels being considered to
have passed down magian secrets to their camel descendents. Do not forget about the camels.

By far and away the most common custom of all these
days of celebration, devotion and contemplation is the
making and eating of breads and cakes. Given how—as we
shall see later—bread and cake form the central component
of some magian grimoiric operations, it seems pertinent to
include a few recipes for various baking projects that can be
offered to the Kings in celebration, and perhaps as tokens
of gratitude for their patronage and protection granted. It
should be noted that this encouragement to bake as a devotional act and to produce a devotional offering is not exactly
convergent with modern Tres Reyes practices: in New
Orleans' expressions of Three Kings customs, for instance,
most Kings' Cake is store-bought. However, I am very satis-
fied—both in terms of historical precedent from various
Books of Secrets and simply as practical Things Magicians
Should Know—to push for more modern grimoiric and
folk necromantic texts to include exploration of spiritual
foodways and material culture via the medium of delicious
dessert recipes.

As much as bread or cake marks a commonality in various magian festivities around the world, the confectionaries
made and how they are used in celebrations are somewhat
specific and differentiated. The French 'Northern style'
Galette des Rois is a round flaky frangipane pastry, whereas
the 'Southern style' *Gateau des Rois* is a brioche-type bread
usually filled or topped with candied fruits and shaped into

A BOOK OF THE MAGI

a crown, and thus also known as *Corona dels Reis*. It is the latter that has obviously influenced the more well-known New Orleans kingcake, which from 1972 also began to include a cinnamon-sugar roll centre.[98] But this crown motif is also found in the Mexican *roscón de reyes* or *rosca de reyes*. These (often oval) crown-shaped breadcake rings frequently share a practice of hiding a trinket inside the cake, representing the Infant Christ. These could be actual porcelain dolls of Jesus but fava beans and other figurines and lucky charms are also used as *la fève*. In France, eating their cakes of the Holy Kings is referred to as when people gather *pour tirer les rois*—to find the kings. Thus the eating of the cake, and the search for the slice which contains the marker of Nazarene, mirrors the Magi's search for the newborn King of Kings. The person who finds the charm is typically considered 'king for a day'—some bakeries even including a paper crown for such a coronation—and this king elected by cake-slice lot must host the next Epiphany party and/or (as found more in Hispanic observances) take the Saviour's figurine to the nearest church on Candlemas. The English tradition of Twelfth (Night) Cakes includes a similar sortilege of the festival's stock characters—Counseller Double Fee, Mrs Prittle Prattle, the Dutchess of Puddle Dock, Toby Tipple and Sir Tun Belly Wash as well as the King and Queen—which are assigned to guests to play for the evening by drawing cards.

But perhaps the best-known Kingcake is that of New Orleans, a crown-style cake topped with icing and coloured sugar, which is typically green, purple, and gold in hon-

---

98 Gil Marks, 'American Cakes—King Cake', Tori Avey. https://toriavey.com/toris-kitchen/king-cake-recipe-history/. Last accessed 12 November 2017.

THE WORKS OF THE THREE HOLY KINGS

our of the cake's links to Mardi Gras. These colours were 'cemented in 1892, when the Rex krewe chose "The Symbolism of Colors" as its theme and put forth the meaning inherent in each hue: justice (purple), faith (green), and wealth (gold)'.[99] The Rex krewe had of course adopted these colours—incidentally those of the Russian Romanov dynasty—from 1875,[100] but it was this later date that secured them as the typical tones for all Epiphany cakes. That is not to say there are not still specific variations: the '"Zulu king cake"—inspired by the Krewe of Zulu, famous since 1910 for passing out coconuts from their floats—features coconut cream filling (or cream cheese mixed with grated coconut) and dark chocolate icing'.[101]

I present here a slightly stripped-down recipe for a relatively 'traditional' Mardis Gras King Cake from food historian Gil Marks.[102]

¶Dough Ingredients

1 package active dry yeast (¼-ounce/7 grams/2¼ teaspoons); 1 cake fresh yeast (0.6-ounce/18 grams); or 2 teaspoons instant yeast

1/4 cup warm water (105 to 115°F for dry yeast; 80 to 85°F for fresh yeast)

1/2 cup warm milk (105 to 115°F for dry yeast; 80 to 85°F for fresh yeast) or sour cream

1/4 cup granulated sugar (1.75 ounces/50 grams)

---

99 Gretchen McKay, 'Mardi Gras: Where Cake is King, and Purple, Green and Gold Reign', *Pittsburgh Post-Gazette*, 22 February 2017. http://www.post-gazette.com/life/food/2017/02/22/Mardi-Gras-Where-cake-is-king-and-purple-green-and-gold-reign/stories/201702220006. Last accessed 12 November 2017.

100 Marks, 'American Cakes—King Cake'.

101 Ibid.

102 Ibid.

1/4 cup unsalted butter, softened (½ stick/2 ounces/57 grams)

2 large egg yolks or 1 large egg

3/4 tsp table salt

1 tsp ground cinnamon or cardamom (optional)

1/2 tsp freshly grated nutmeg (optional)

1/8 tsp almond extract (optional)

1 tsp grated lemon zest (optional)

2 tsp grated orange zest or orange blossom water (optional)

2 1/4 cups unbleached all-purpose flour or bread flour (9.5 ounces/275 grams)

1/4-1/2 cup chopped candied citron, ½ cup chopped mixed candied fruit, or ½ cup golden raisins (5 ounces/140 grams)

Egg wash (1 large egg beaten with 1 teaspoon milk or water)

¶Icing Ingredients

1 cup confectioners' sugar (4 ounces/115 grams)

2 tbsp unsalted butter, softened (¼ stick/1 ounce/28 grams) (or ¼ cup cream cheese, softened (2 ounces/57 grams) (optional))

1/2 tsp vanilla extract or ¼ teaspoon almond extract

1 tbsp milk, buttermilk, fresh lemon juice, or water

a few drops gold food coloring or 2 to 4 tablespoons yellow colored sugar (optional)

a few drops green food coloring or 2 to 4 tablespoons green colored sugar (optional)

a few drops purple food coloring or 2 to 4 tablespoons purple colored sugar (optional)

THE WORKS OF THE THREE HOLY KINGS

¶Instructions

In a small bowl or measuring cup, dissolve the yeast in the water. Stir in 1 teaspoon sugar and let stand until foamy, 5 to 10 minutes.

In a large bowl, combine the yeast mixture, milk, sugar, butter, egg yolks, salt, and, for a flavored dough (but omit this if you are using a filling), the spice or zest.

Blend in 1½ cups flour.

Gradually add enough of the remaining flour to make a soft workable dough.

On a lightly floured surface or in a mixer with a dough hook, knead the dough until smooth and springy, about 5 minutes.[103]

Knead in the citron, mixed candied fruit or golden raisins.

Place in an oiled bowl and turn to coat. Cover with a kitchen towel or loosely with plastic wrap and let rise in a warm, draft-free place until doubled in bulk, about 2 hours, or in the refrigerator overnight

[Punch down the dough and briefly knead again.]

---

103 I have personally found that this recipe requires a fair bit more flour to get to optimal dough texture.

A BOOK OF THE MAGI

Position a rack in the center of the oven. Preheat the oven to 350°F.

[Roll the dough out and form it into a ring, pinching the ends]

Place on a parchment paper-lined or greased baking sheet, seam side down. Cover with a towel or plastic wrap spritzed with cooking spray and let rise at room temperature until nearly doubled in bulk, about 1 hour.

Brush the dough with the egg wash.

To make the icing: in a medium bowl, stir the confectioners' sugar, optional butter or cream cheese, vanilla, and enough milk until smooth and of a pouring consistency.

If desired, divide the icing into thirds and tint each third with one of the food colorings. Or you can drizzle or spread the icing over the warm cake.

While the icing is still wet, sprinkle with the colored sugar. Decorating a King Cake neatly can be tricky, it is quite a messy process! We found the easiest way to do this neatly is to use a pastry brush to apply icing to each section, then sprinkle with sugar, let dry, and move on to the next section.

Serve warm or at room temperature. After cooling, the cake can be wrapped well in plastic, then foil and stored at room temperature for up to 5 days or in the freezer

THE WORKS OF THE THREE HOLY KINGS

for up to 3 months. Do not cover with the icing before freezing.

Marks also presents several variations: from instructions in how to produce a braided version of the cake, to a recipe for the newer cinnamon-roll form of king cake. Any of these are suitable to make for Epiphany, and I have found they are well received out-of-season as devotional offerings: again, these can be presented at your altar and even left at three-way crossroads, which are traditionally associated with the Magi.

Prayers to the Three Kings

O Almighty Creator of the Heavens, who revealed thy incarnation by the testimony of a bright heavenly star, which seeing, the Magi adored thy Majesty with the offering of gifts: in thanksgiving therefore, I offer thee the sacrifice of praise and graciously beseech thee to grant to me that in my mind the star of righteousness may always appear, and that my treasure may be confessing thee, Lord Jesus Christ. Amen.[104]

This prayer comes to us from the *Book of Cerne*, an Anglo-Saxon Latin personal prayer book thought to have been compiled in Mercia in the early ninth century. It introduces

---

104 Quoted in Mountney, *The Three Holy Kings of Cologne*, vii.

A BOOK OF THE MAGI

us to the historiolae central to magian devotion—those of the Journey (by the light of the Star) and the Adoration. Once more, we are reminded that Magi adore the majesty and not necesssarily the incarnate godhead of the Infant. In praying it, the speaker draws strength from the example set by the Three Kings: as they gave gifts, so too do we give honour and worship. This praise is itself considered as a 'sacrifice', of our time and of our breath and of our attention. Indeed, this mindfulness is somewhat expressly enchanted, as we ask for 'the star of righteousness'—either one *like* that which guided the magi or the *very same one*—to light our way, to herald our path and our actions.

These simple but powerful technical dimensions of magian prayer are expounded upon in following prayer found in the fourteenth-century manuscript now labelled MS Harley 2253. This document attests the only known version of this particular orison, which its editors and translators describe as an 'elegant Anglo-Norman prayer to the Three Kings':

I entreat you, Jaspar, Melchior, and Balthazar, crowned kings, who went to seek Jesus when he was born of the Virgin Mary, for that sweetness you felt toward him when you went to seek him, and for that joy you felt when you found him and offered him your gifts, that you advise me regarding that which I ask you inasmuch as God hears you and accepted your gifts. True God, as you accepted their gifts, may you accept today my prayer on account of their love; and as the star appeared to them in the east, which led them to you in the place they had so greatly desired, so too, Lord God, you filled my desire for gladness and joy. Grant me that I may

62

THE WORKS OF THE THREE HOLY KINGS

have and behold what my heart desires, for the praise of God and my Lady Saint Mary. Amen.[105]

Susanna Fein *et al.* break the prayer down thusly: 'It first addresses the Magi in honor of their desire to give to God and how God so readily accepted their gifts. From there, the petitioner turns his address to God, asking that God likewise accept this prayer as a gift and fill the petitioner with gifts of gladness and joy'.[106] Let us briefly examine the several layers cited from our familiar story in more technical depth.

Firstly, the emphasis on gladness and especially joy should be contextualised by the *Golden Legend* reading finding the Magi prophesied in the deuterocanonical Book of Baruch. The *Golden Legend* establishes a fivefold comprehension of the appearance of the Star, and emphasises how sequential understanding of these five levels of understanding produce epiphanies specifically in the modality of joy. Each of the stages or forms of the Star is afforded a specific interpretation that identifies a particular beat of their mythic cycle, and interrelates them into further Christian mysteries. They are also emphasised to apply previous prophecy to the Adoration, thus connecting it to an older mythic source:

Seeing the star, they rejoiced with exceeding great joy. Note that the star the Magi saw was a fivefold star—a material, a spiritual, an intellectual, a rational, and a su-

---

105 MS Harley 2253, art. 108a, f. 135v. I am very grateful to my colleague and friend Daniel Harms for bringing this prayer to my attention.

106 *The Complete Harley Manuscript 2253: Volume 3*, ed. and trans. Susanna Fein with David Raybin and Jan Ziolkowski (Western Michigan University: Medieval Institute Publications, 2015), 354.

A BOOK OF THE MAGI

persubstantial star. The first star, the material star, they saw in the East. The spiritual star, which is faith, they saw in their hearts, for if this star of faith had not shone in their hearts, they never would have come to the vision of that first star... The third, the intellectual star, is the angel they saw in sleep, when they were warned by an angel not to go back to Herod... The fourth, the rational star, was the Blessed Virgin, whom they saw with the Child. The superstantial star, which was Christ himself, they saw in the manger, and of these two last stars we read: 'Entering into the house they found the Child with Mary his Mother'. Each of these five is called 'the star'. Thus the first, Ps. 8:4: 'The moon and the stars which thou hast founded'; the second, Ecclus. 43:10: 'the glory of the stars (i.e., of the virtues) is the beauty of heaven (i.e., of the celestial man)'; the third, Bar. 3:34: 'the stars have given light in their watches and rejoiced'; the fourth in the hymn *Are maris stella*; the fifth, Apoc. 22:16: 'I am the root and stock of David, the bright and morning star'.

At the sight of the first and second of these stars the Magi rejoiced. Seeing the third, they rejoiced with joy. The sight of the fourth made them rejoice with great joy, and of the fifth, with exceeding great joy.[107]

There are also vitally significant technical dimensions that should be examined in this Harley prayer. Just as the adoration of the Christ-child by the Magi is taken as a central exemplar for our own adoring of Godhead, so too is the

107 *Golden Legend*, 1:82.

THE WORKS OF THE THREE HOLY KINGS

Saviour's acceptance of their gifts suggested as a sign or hopeful precedent that our prayers will be accepted. Furthermore, the Journey of our three kings is explicitly framed as a historiola for the striving towards and eventual fulfilment of *what our hearts desire.* This last point renders this a most suitable prayer to include in both devotional and more expressly sorcerous workings.

A Work of Healing

Take the blode of the littel fynger of hym that is seke and wryte thir thre names in his forhed of the iij kynges of Colayn, that is to say: Jasper fert aurum, thus Melchior, Attro pamirram. he that beris thir names of thir iij kyngis with hym, he sall be lesid thurgh the petee of God of the falland evyll. Or write tham with the sam blode & hynge tham abowt his nek in a writ.[108]

This work of healing involves the first instance of the use of blood we have thus encountered. This is a feature of several magian operations, and perhaps speaks as much to standards in medieval and early modern magic as it does to specifically magian mysteries. What is significant to note is that in every operation under the auspices of the Three

---

108 Found in the *Liber de Diversis Medicinis* copied into the Lincoln Cathedral Thornton MS. Quoted in Julia Boffey, '"Many grete myraclys... in divers contreys of the eest': The Reading and Circulation of the Middle English Prose *Three Kings of Cologne'*, in *Medieval Women: Texts and Contexts in Late Medieval Britain. Essays for Felicity Riddy*, ed. J. Wogan-Browne *et al.* (Brepols: Turnhout, 2000), 39. Cited in Williamson, 168.

A BOOK OF THE MAGI

Kings, the blood is used to write—whether the names of the Magi themselves, the names of spirits, or (as in this case) magical formulae. As we shall see, the charm itself ('Jasper fert...' etc) is far from unique to this healing spell or amulet. Nor is the appeal to the Three Kings against the 'falling evil', which usually connotes epilepsy.

Perhaps the most unique element of this working is the name of the third Magi—'Attro'—which seems at odds with our standard three-piece outfit. Williamson identifies a couple of talismanic objects in the material history of the Three Kings which suggest there was some sort of tradition of the third being called Attro or even Atropa, the name of the third of the Moirai or Fates.[109] But this connection between the Kings and the Fates is far from clear, and remains a mystery to be further explored, terrain still to be journeyed...

||||||||||||||||||||||||||||||||||||||||||||||||||||||||||||||||||||||||||||||||||||||||||||||||

The Grimoiric Record

The following appearances of the Three Kings—culled from early modern grimoiric texts—combine *materia* with written, spoken, gestural, and offertory components and processes collectively thought to efficiently gather and transmit the occult virtues of the Three Magi in order to achieve specific effects. It behoves us to examine the weight and substance of these ingredients and actions—both to develop a deeper understanding and engagement with such workings, and to potentially explore new yet traditionally

109 Williamson, 168–69.

rooted ways to work. I intend to highlight a stock of techniques, materials, and actions that might be considered a sort of Three Kingly storehouse of their totemic ingredients and means of working. I also offer brief commentary and analysis mainly in order to demonstrate how such ritual design aspects might be responsibly developed and deployed in one's practice. My intention is not to armchair out all the possible ways one could build rituals for the Three Kings so much as show (rather than tell) how to pull out details, follow threads, and structure the work of ritual design, devotional practice, and magical operation.

Workings of Strength and Endurance

¶Not To Tire Of Walking

Write on three silk ribbons, *Gaspar, Melchior, Balthazard*. Tie one of the ribbons above the right knee[110] without tightening it; the second above the left knee[111] and the third around the small of the back.[112] Before setting off, swallow a small glass of aniseed in some broth or in a glass of white wine, and rub your feet with some crushed rue in olive oil.[113]

Grimoire of Honorius (Rome, 1760), f. 66–67; in Rankine and Barron (eds.), 156.

---

110 *Black Dragon*: `below the right knee'. *Crossed Keys*, 59.

111 *BD*: `below the left knee'. *Crossed Keys*, 59.

112 *BD*: `about the waist'. *Crossed Keys*, 59.

113 *BD*: `rub your feet with dust from the street steeped in olive oil'. *Crossed Keys*, 59.

A BOOK OF THE MAGI

In such an operation we have a combination of material components (aniseed, broth/white wine, rue, and olive oil) with textual talismanic objects (the three named silk ribbons), points of bodily focus (the knees, the small of the back, the feet), as well as an ordered sequence of observances. It would benefit practitioners to explore the wider and deeper meaning of rue, for instance. One might well benefit from experimentation with different methodologies for writing upon the ribbons (for instance, different inks and pens), as well as attempting the operation in various planetary hours. Finally, the rubbing of the feet may well suggest a practice of anointing the parts of the body pertinent to work ahead of us: on our eyes before engaging in long bouts of reading, for instance. The feet might also be considered foundational to enchanting ourselves, 'what we stand upon', and rites of anointing them with other substances might also fall under the auspices of our patron Magi.

I must also point out the use, in this spell's alternate version in the *Black Dragon*, of dust from the street. The use of dirts, soils and dusts from particular locations in Western occult philosophy is generally discussed more in light of visiting places to charge talismans—as when Agrippa recommends burying love amulets in or near brothels.[114] Here, we do not simply visit and work a point of particular envirtued locales—we bring the materia back and prepare it as an oil.

---

114 'they that endeavor to procure love, are wont to bury for a certain time the instruments of their art, whether they be rings, images, looking-glasses, or any other, to hide them in a stew house, because in that place they will contract some venerall faculty, no otherwise then things that stand in stinking places, become stinking, and those in an Aromaticall place, become Aromaticall, and of a sweet favour'. Heinrich C. Agrippa, *Three Books of Occult Philosophy* (London, 1651), 96.

THE WORKS OF THE THREE HOLY KINGS

¶Garter In Order To Travel Without Tiring Oneself
Leave your house whilst fasting, walk on the left-hand
side until you have found a merchant of ribbons. Buy an
ell of white ribbon. Pay what is asked of you and leave a
farthing behind in the shop[115] and return home by the
same path. The next day, do the same until you have
found a merchant of feathers. Buy a quantity of them,[116]
in the same manner that you bought the ribbon. And
when you are back in your dwelling, with your own
blood, write the characters ['from fig. 3, plate II'] on the
ribbon for the right garter. Those of the third line are
for the left. When this has been done, leave the house.
On the third day, wear your ribbon and your feather,
walk on the left-hand side until you find a confectioner
or a baker. Buy a cake or a two farthing loaf of bread.
Go to the first tavern and ask for a quarter of a pint of
wine,[117] have the glass rinsed three times by the same
person, break the cake or the bread into three pieces
and put the three pieces into the glass with the wine.
Take the first piece and throw it under the table without looking, saying *Irly, for thee*. Then take the second
piece and throw it, saying *Terly, for thee*. On the other
side of the garter, write the names of these two Spirits
with your blood. Throw the third piece, saying *Firly, for
thee*. Throw the feather away, drink the wine without
eating, pay your share of the bill and leave. When you

115 In the operation listed in the Marvellous Secrets of the *Black Dragon*, it is speci-
fied 'Pay the amount he asks, letting a farthing fall in the Shop'. *Crossed Keys*, 58.
116 In the Marvellous Secrets of the *Black Dragon*: 'buy a trimmed one'. *Crossed
Keys*, 58.
117 In the Marvellous Secrets of the *Black Dragon*: 'half a pint of wine'. *Crossed Keys*,
59.

A BOOK OF THE MAGI

Grimoire of Honorius (Rome, 1760), f. 51–53; in Rankine and Barron, eds., p. 144–45.

are outside the town, put on your garters. Take care not to make any mistake by placing the garter for the right leg on the left, as there will be consequences. Strike the earth three times with your foot, while calling on the names of the Spirits, *Irly, Terly, Balthazard, Melchior, Gaspard, let us go.*[118] Then go on your journey.

This is of course a rather more involved rite than the last, yet has as its basis the same goal. It certainly extensively develops the actions and components of the former operation. We are given the colour and means of acquiring the ribbons, as well as a timing, location, ink, and manner for marking them. We can also note some commonalities between the two workings—such as how the right ribbon seems to be prepared first. We might also note the recurrence of drinking wine. Indeed, a whole variety of food-ways are presented: from fasting to the use of bread or cake. Certainly, the Christian undertones of this act of breaking bread should not be overlooked.

Differences between this and the previous operation include no mention of the third ribbon for the back, and of course the naming and offerings made to the attendant spirits Irly, Terly, and Firly. We are given a location to find them or at least petition them—inns being under the three kings particular patronage as we should remember—and the manner in which their offerings are made. It seems these spirits, along with the Magi, are considered to accompany the traveller on their journey. We are advised to write in our blood upon the offerings given—if indeed the bread or cake pieces should even be seen as offerings. It is pertinent

118 In the Marvellous Secrets of the *Black Dragon*: 'let's walk!' *Crossed Keys*, 59.

THE WORKS OF THE THREE HOLY KINGS

to note that the combination of cake-bread and wine itself evokes the transformative and purifying rites of the Mass of course.

In terms of embodiment, this second anti-fatigue working introduces fasting as an operative practice, as well as the use of one's own blood. It also once more highlights the significance of the feet—in this case, stamping them. We should be aware of both the embodied location of a magian power in the feet, and also of the embodied experience of weariness that stamping can produce—the feet are made to feel fatigued in an experiential historiola further conjoining operator and mythic focus. To cement or foreground this dimension, I find employing Isaiah 40:31 as a psalm-style charm very suitable for such purposes: *But they that wait upon the LORD shall renew their strength; they shall mount up with wings as eagles; they shall run, and not be weary; and they shall walk, and not faint.* The ritually generated weariness of stamped feet becomes a testament, a qualification, and a protection proclaiming: I will grow no wearier than this.

Speaking more broadly of additions or developments or further experimentations of such spellcraft, while one could view the second of these operations as more 'complete' for having more details, the existence of the first should not, I contend, be taken as a mere simplification or suffering from omissions. Rather we might see the former as a barebones working and the latter as a specific instantiation of the general rite.

✞ ✞ ✞

A Work of Detection

¶An Experiment of Two Hazel Rods of
     One Year's Growth

Note that the rods be but of one year's growth and not
above, because that if they be there will be a fault in the
operation. When thou wilt gather them, let it be upon
the first Friday of the Moon before the Sun rising, in
saying 'In the name of the Holy Ghost, I do cut thee',
either of them at four strokes, and that being done, say,
'*In principio erat verbum*, etc.', which being said, say three
Pater Nosters, in the honour of the Trinity, seven *Ave
Marias*, in the honour of the seven joys of Mary the Virgin. Then say, 'O Lord by whose providence mankind
is increased, and all things have their being, humbly we
beseech thee to put away from us all hurtful things, and
that thou wilt grant to us that all things may be brought
to good pass that we take in hand, through Jesus Christ
our Lord. Amen'.

> *In Nomine Patris, Filii, et Spiritus Sancti*. Amen. Lord,
> hear my prayer and let cry come unto thee. Let us
> pray. O Lord, by whose providence the earth and all
> therein was created, grant grace to these, thy crea-
> tures, that they may be unto me aiding, both now
> and at all other times as when I shall have cause to
> use them, so that the rather by them I may come
> to the knowledge of that thing I desire. This grant,
> good lord, I do beseech thee for they dear Son Jesus
> Christ's sake. Amen.

THE WORKS OF THE THREE HOLY KINGS

This being said, say:

> I conjure you, hazel rods of one year's growing this
> day, by the ineffable names of God + Hely + Hely-
> son + Orca + Tetragrammaton + that you bring
> me without all manner of deceit and craft unto the
> place where any treasure is hidden, or any other
> thing, and that by virtue of the hole name of God
> written in you. I command you that you do not rule
> in vain. I adjure you, O hazels of one year's growth,
> by the three kings of Cullen, Jasper, Melchior, and
> Balthazar, that, as they being wise and prudent
> men, were conducted and led by a star where as they
> found Christ, that so you may bring me into the
> certain and sure place where any treasure is or metal
> is hid or hath any being, and that this be done. I
> bid and command you by the power of God the
> Father, who hath made you, by God the Son, who
> hath redeemed me, and by the Holy Spirit who hath
> sanctified me and all creatures. Amen. Amen.

In the first rod, write arifax + Agla + three times. In the
other, write + Adonay + three Raavarax times.

Vb.26, f.
140; in
*Book of
Oberon,*
363-64.

The warning about using hazel rods no older than a year
reminds us of grimoiric instructions to use woods that have
not yet borne fruit—itself very reminiscent of notions of the
power *in potentia* of 'virgin' materials. Given the divinatory
intentions of the rods' magical preparation or cultivation in
this manner, this potency of virginity should also remind
us of the prevalence, or at least perceived efficacy, of child
seers throughout the history and practice of magic. It also

A BOOK OF THE MAGI

of course brings to mind the Blessed Virgin Mary: arguably the second most important figure in the crèche scenes into which the Magi find themselves so popularly formulated.

In terms of the potential for spirit-work within this operation, the rods themselves are treated as creatures whom God sanctifies and whom the magician must conjure. The Three Kings are specifically mentioned as being 'of Cullen' (aka Cologne aka Köln), offering not only historicity (as attested in the survey that formed the first part of this book), but a physical and mythic location from which we might further engage our patrons. Liturgically, the mention of the Seven Joys affords Marian devotional approaches to support such work. For those of us who could do with a reminder, the Seven Joys are:

The Annunciation.
The Nativity of Jesus.
The Adoration of the Magi.
The Resurrection of Christ.
The Ascension of Christ to Heaven.
The Pentecost or Descent of the Holy Spirit upon the Apostles and Mary.
The Coronation of the Virgin in Heaven.

It is tempting to see this operation as little more than a means to consecrate treasure-hunting tools, and certainly it seems this was the utility at the foremost of the author's mind. Just as the Magi searched for the Christ-child, so we may search for the gold of the earth; indeed, this formula of precedent is to be explicitly ritually stated. Yet we should bear in mind that the operation can also be performed to lead us to 'any other thing', and various other detection applications present themselves. Moreover, we can I believe consider the 'search for truth' as a fair reading of the Journey and Adoration, and thus the rods' use in divination in general begins to look more appealing.

In terms of wider applications of this operation's components, this operation presents a prayer battery of specifically numbered Our Fathers and Hail Marys, as well as a set of divine names that might well be employed in other workings.

Works of Protection

¶Against the Falling-Evill
...this ensuing is another counterfeit Charm of theirs, whereby the Falling-evil is presently remedied.

Gaspar fert myrrham, thus Melchior, Balthasar aurum,
Haec tria qui secum portabit nomina regum,
Solvitur à morbo Christi pietate caduco.
Gasper with his myrrh began
These presents to unfold,
Then Melchior brought in Frankincense,
And Balthasar brought in Gold.
Now he that of these holy Kings
The Names about shall bear,
The falling ill by grace of Christ
Shall never need to fear.

> The effects are too good to be true in such a patched piece of Popery.

This is a true copy of the Holy-writing, that was brought down from Heaven by an Angel to S. Leo, Pope of Rome;

and he did bid him take it to King Charles, when he went
to the battel at Ronceval. And the Angel said, that what
man or woman beareth this writing about them with good
devotion, and saith every day three Pater-nosters, three
Aves, and one Creed, shall not that day be overcome or his
Enemies, either bodily or ghostly; neither shall be robbed or
slain of Theeves, Pestilence, Thunder, or Lightning, neither
shall be hurt with fire or water, nor cumbred with Spirits,
neither shall he have displeasure of Lords or Ladies: he
shall not be condemned with false witness, nor taken with
Fairies, or any manner of Axes, nor yet with the Falling-
evil. Also, if a woman be in Travel, lay this writing upon her
belly, she shall have easie deliverance, and the child right
shape and Christendom, and the mother Purification of
holy Church, and all through vertue of these holy Names of
Jesus Christ following:

✠ Jesus ✠ Christus ✠ Messias ✠ Soter ✠ Emmanuel ✠
Sabbath ✠ Adonai ✠ Unigenitus ✠ Majestas ✠ Para-
cletus ✠ Salvatur noster ✠ Agiros iskiros ✠ Agios ✠
Adonatos ✠ Gasper ✠ Melchior ✠ & Balthasar ✠ Mat-
thaeus ✠ Marcios ✠ Lucos ✠ Johannes.

The Epistle of S. Saviour, which Pope Leo sent to King
Charles, saying, that whosoever carrieth the same about
him, or in what day soever he shall read it, or shall
see it, he shall not be killed with any Iron-tool, nor be
burned with fire, nor be drowned with water, neither
any evil man or other creature may hurt him. The Cross
of Christ is a wonderful defence ✠ the cross of Christ
be alwayes with me ✠ the cross is it which I do always
worship ✠ the cross of Christ is true health ✠ the cross

THE WORKS OF THE THREE HOLY KINGS

of Christ doth lose the bands of death ✙ the cross of
Christ is the truth and the way ✙ I take my journey
upon the cross of the Lord ✙ the cross of Christ beareth
down every evil ✙ the cross of Christ giveth all good
things ✙ the cross of Christ taketh away pains everlast-
ing ✙ the cross of Christ save me ✙ O cross of Christ
be upon me, before me, and behind me ✙ because the
ancient Enemy cannot abide the sight of thee ✙ the
cross of Christ save me, keep me, govern me, and direct
me ✙ Thomas bearing this note of thy divine Majesty ✙
Alpha ✙ Omega ✙ first ✙ and last ✙ midst ✙ and end
✙ beginning ✙ first begotten ✙ wisdom ✙ vertue ✙.

Scot, *Dis-
covery of
Witchcraft*
(London,
1584: 1665
edition),
130-31.

As promised, this operation bears much similarity with the
previously mentioned medieval charm or textual amulet—the same written component, the same ends, the same
utility. Yet this version seems to have grown in power, or
at least contains reference to far more specific protective
and curative properties. Scot attempts to cite the extent
of the exact claims of this charms' protection as grounds
for its dismissal—it is far 'too good to be true'. Such claims
might themselves be magnified to serve anti-Papish efforts
to discredit such charms' users as gullible. However, even
setting aside the exact parameters of the charm's effects and
effectiveness, it is clearly a protective item which shields
the user against more than 'the falling-evil'. To categorise
the extensive claims of Scot's source, the charm offers
physical safety against natural disasters, and against those
who would wish harm to one's body and reputation. It also
guards against being haunted, kidnapped or otherwise
encumbered by spirits.

We can observe from its employment in easing labour

77

that the magical operation is performed, like the anti-
fatigue ribbons, by applying a written charm to a pertinent
area of the human body. We can also infer the importance
of the charm being seen by both the magician and those
who wish ill to that operator. Far from being hidden on
one's person, the charm—like the cross of Christ—should
be beheld. In mentioning the midwifery aid of this charm,
I also cannot help but note the similarity of the word
'travel'—an obvious mythic feature of the Magi's purview,
addressed in the travellers' workings above—with that of
'travail' or childbirth, itself a less obvious but nevertheless
still highly pertinent feature of the foundational legend of
the Three Kings searching—the quest for a newborn.

There is an alternative and far briefer version of this
working:

¶For Epilepsy
Exhale into the right ear of the one who has had an epi-
leptic fit saying these words: *Gaspar fert myrrbam, thus
Melchior, Baltazar aurum.* The patient should recover
immediately, and to heal utterly from the condition, it is
necessary to take three iron nails the length of his little
finger and hammer them into the place he suffered his
first fit whilst saying over each the name of the patient.

Marvel-
lous
Secrets in
*The Black
Dragon*
(*Crossed
Keys*, 199)

On a simple reflection upon 'why epilepsy', it is tempting to
look to the kneeling as an instance of controlled or deliberate falling, as an act of obeisance and devotion, as opposed
to the uncontrollable of weaknesses and falls brought about
by this condition. Regardless, here the disease itself is
nailed down, by working the place at which it first mani-
fested. It is tempting to see this as a form of 'time-travel'—of

comprehending occult contagion across and through place and time, of returning the illness from the named patient to its source or point of transference. It also seems pertinent to raise the practice of casting a *decumbiture* in pre-modern medical diagnosis and prognostication, by which the nature of the disease could be determined by setting a particular sort of horary astrological chart: specifically a snapshot of the heavens at the moment the disease first struck or made itself known. Knowing the roots of a condition—whether in temporally or (as in this operation's case) geographically could provide the means by which one could manipulate it.

¶Against the biting of a Mad-Dog
Put a silver Ring on the finger, within the which these words are graven

J. Bodinus lib. de daemon. 3. cap. 5.

✝ Habay ✝ habar ✝ hebar ✝

and say to the person bitten with a mad Dog, *I am thy Saviour, lose not thy life*: and then prick him in the nose thrice, that at each time he bleed. Otherwise, take Pills made of the skull of one that is hanged. Otherwise: write upon a piece of bread, *Irioni, khïriora, esser, khuder, feres*; and let it be eaten by the party bitten. Otherwise,

O Rex gloriae Jesu Christe, veni cum pace: In nomine Patris max. in nomine Filii max. in nomine Spiritus sancti prax. Gasper, Melchior, Balthasar ✝ prax ✝ max ✝ Deus I max ✝.

But in troth this is very dangerous; insomuch as if it be not speedily and cunningly prevented, either death

A BOOK OF THE MAGI

or phrensie insueth, through infection of the humor left in the wound bitten by a mad Dog: which because bad Chirurgians cannot cure, they have therefore used foolish cosening Charms. But Dodonaeus in his Herbal saith, that the herb Alysson cureth it: which experiment, I doubt not, will prove more true then all the Charms in the world. But where he saith, *That the same hanged at a mans Gate or Entry, preserveth him and his Cattel from Inchantment, or bewitching,* he is overtaken with folly.

Scot,
*Discovery
of Witch-
craft*, 137

Here the names of the Magi are included in rather more general appeals to heal or otherwise deliver a patient from death or frenzy (which presumably refers more to rabies than impassioned *exstasis*). If we were looking for a themat-ically apt meaning to this deliverance, I suggest we consider that the Magi deliver gifts. And of course, as already men-tioned above, delivery is also a duty of midwives.

Once more, a piece of bread is employed, this time as the vehicle for the consumption of the *voces magicae* to ef-fect a cure. This recurring motif or technique seems to sug-gest the ingestion of various other magical writings upon bread for other purposes. The ring is also reminiscent of the 'cramp-rings' mentioned earlier in that the words are to be 'graven within', i.e., inscribed on the inside. The methods of cure preceding the invocation of the Three Kings in this charm might be taken to have some further connection with the Magi; certainly the use of a human skull is tempting to explore further in light of working the Magi in necroman-tic manners as I am suggesting. But we might equally take the appeal to Gaspar *et al.* as a last resort, a final option, reserved because of its severity, or simply as an alternate approach after the failure of the previous attempts.

|||||||||||||||||||||||||||||||||||||||||||||||||||||||||||||||||||||||||||||||||||||

Works of Conjuration

*Extract of conjuration for 'any spirit, or spirits, as hereafter fol-
loweth, first thou shalt turn thy face into the east and say thus',*

> ... I conjure you, by the power and belief of the three
> kings that offered to Christ Jesus our lord and saviour
> and by that which they offered and by the names, and
> by the sound of the names as these, Jaspar ✛ Melchior
> ✛ Balthazar ✛ and by all good and faithful men and
> women and by all their beliefs that they have in God
> and his works. Also I conjure you and adjure you and
> b[ind?] you, by all the kings of the air, and of the earth
> and water and fire, and air of hell, that you go from
> this ground, and that you leave the treasure here where
> it stands, and that you, not none of you, not no other
> spirit or spirits carry it not from us, nor turn it not into
> no other likeness or fashion. Also I conjure and bind
> you all spirits and elves and men, beast and all dogs that
> none of you do away or let us, by God the maker and
> redeemer of all things both visible and unvisible, and by
> his wounds and hairs, sinews, and veins, I charge you by
> the blessed Trinity, three persons and one God omnipo-
> tent and celestial, without beginning and shall be God
> without end. [Amen.]

Folger
Vb26 f.
220; *Book
of Oberon*,
521.

We begin with a charge by the 'power and belief' that the
Magi offered to the Infant, once more highlighting the
operative effects of devotion. This conjuration moreover
seems to suggest the speaking or 'sound' as well as the writing of the Magi's names has operative virtue. The idea of a

conjuration that can bind 'any spirit/s' is certainly useful, and this universality appears to be supported by the appeals to the kings of every element, and the infernal kings of 'the air of hell' for good measure. This last kingship is especially pertinent to comprehending newer Christian demonology's adaptations of older notion of aerial daimones. We also have the inclusion of 'elves' alongside spirits, beasts, and men, highlighting faerie as a distinct class of beings in the wider cosmology within which this conjuration operates. In this we can perhaps detect a spirit-working application of Psalm 72's injunction that kings shall bow. Likewise, in this conjuration we find an overt Christian interpretation of the Magi in terms of the Trinity—like the Adoration, we are encouraged to meditate on the concept of 'three persons and one God'.

¶An Experiment of Bealphares
This is proved the noblest carrier that ever did serve any man upon the earth, and here beginneth the inclosing of the said Spirit, and how to have a true answer of him, without any craft or harm; and he will appear unto thee in the likeness of a fair man or fair woman, the which Spirit will come to thee at all times. And if thou wilt command him to tell thee of hidden treasures that be in any place, he will tell it thee: or if thou wilt command him to bring to thee gold or silver, he will bring it thee: or if thou wilt go from one Countrey to another, he will bear thee without any harm of body or soul. Therefore he that will do this work, shall abstain from lecherousness and drunkenness, and from false swearing, and do all the abstinence that he may do, and namely three days before he go to work, and in the third day when the

THE WORKS OF THE THREE HOLY KINGS

night is come, and when the Starrs do shine, and the element fair and clear, he shall bath himself and his fellows (if he have any) all together in a quick well-spring; Then he must be cloathed in clean white cloathes; and he must have another privy place, and bear him ink and pen, wherewith he shall write this holy Name of God Almighty in his right hand ✝ 𝕬𝖌𝖑𝖆 ✝ and in his left hand this name ✝ ⅠⅠ ℂ ▽ ℂ ✝ and he must have a dry thong of a Lions or of a Harts skin, and make thereof a girdle, and write the holy names of God all about, and in the end ✝ A & Ω. ✝ And upon his brest he must have this present figure or mark written in Virgin Parchment, as it is here shewed.

And it must be sowed upon a piece of new linnen, and so made fast upon thy brest. And if thou wilt have a fellow to work with thee, he must be appointed in the same manner. You must have also a bright knife that was never occupied, and he must write

✝ ✝ ✝
𝕳𝖔𝖒𝖔 𝖘𝖆𝖈𝖆𝖗𝖚𝖘,
𝖒𝖚𝖘𝖊𝖔 𝖑𝖔𝖒𝖊𝖆𝖘,
𝖈𝖍𝖊𝖗𝖚𝖇𝖔𝖟𝖈𝖆
✝

on the one side of the blade of the knife ✝ 𝕬𝖌𝖑𝖆 ✝ and on the otherside of the knifes blade ✝ ⅠⅠ ℂ ▽ ℂ ✝ And with the same knife he must make a circle, as hereafter followeth: the which is called Solomons circle. When that is made, go into the circle, and close again the place, there where thou wentest in, with the same knife, and say; Per crucis hoc signum ✝ fugiat procul omne malignum; Et per idem signum ✝ salbetur quodque

A BOOK OF THE MAGI

benigum; *By the sign of the Cross ✠ may all evil fly farre away, and by the same sign ✠ may all that is good be preserved;* and make suffumigations to thy self, and to thy fellow or fellows, with Frankincense, Mastick, Lignum Aloes: then put it in Wine, and say with good devotion, in the worship of the high God Almighty, all together, that he may defend you from all evils. And when he that is Master will close the Spirit, he shall say towards the East with meek and devout devotion, these Psalms and Prayers as followeth here in order.

Memorandum that you must read the 22. and 51 Psalm all over; or else rehearse them by heart, for these are counted necessary, &c.

¶The two and twentieth Psalm
*O My God my God, look upon me, why hast thou forsaken me, and art so farr from my health, and from the words of my complaint? * And so forth to the end of the same Psalm, as it is to be found in the Book.

This Psalm also following, being the fifty one Psalm, must be said three times over, &c.

Have mercy upon me, O God, after thy great goodness, according to the multitude of thy mercies, do away mine offences. And so forth to the end of the same Psalm, concluding it with, *Glory to the Father, and to the Son, and to the Holy Ghost; As it was in the beginning, is now and ever shall be, world without end, Amen.* Then say this verse: *O Lord leave not my soul with the wicked; nor my life with the blood-thirsty.* Then say a *Pater noster*, an *Ave Maria*, and a *Credo & Ne nos inducas. O Lord shew us thy mercy, and we shall be saved. Lord hear our prayer, and let our cry come unto thee.* Let us pray.

THE WORKS OF THE THREE HOLY KINGS

*O Lord God Almighty, as thou warnedst by thine Angel,
the three Kings of Cullen, Jasper, Melchior, and Balthasar,
when they came with worshipful presents toward Bethelem;
Jasper brought myrrh; Melchior, incense; Balthasar, gold;
worshipping the high King of all the world, Jesus Gods Son
of Heaven, the second Person in Trinity, being born of the
holy and clean Virgin S. Mary Queen of Heaven, Empress of
Hell, and Lady of all the world: at that time the holy Angel
Gabriel warned and bad the foresaid three Kings, that they
should take another way, for dread of peril, that Herod the
King by his Ordinance would have destroyed these three
Noble Kings, that meekly sought out our Lord and Saviour.
As wittily and truly as these three Kings turned for dread,
and took another way; so wisely and so truly, O Lord God,
of thy mightiful mercy, bless us now at this time, for thy
blessed passion save us, and keep us all together from all
evil; and thy holy Angel defend us.*

Let us pray.

Gaspar, Balthasar, and Melchior, who followed the Star,
wherein was the image of a little Babe bearing a cross is
Longa lagenda Colonia; lie not

*O Lord, King of all Kings, which containest the Throne of
Heavens, and beholdest all deeps, weighest the hills, and
shuttest up with thy hand the earth, hear us most meek God,
and grant unto us (being unworthy) according to thy great
mercy, to have the verity and vertue of knowledge of hidden
treasure by this Spirit invocated, through thy help O Lord
Jesus Christ, to whom be all honour and glory, from worlds
to worlds everlastingly, Amen.*

A BOOK OF THE MAGI

Then say these names,

✝ Helie ✝ Helion ✝ essejere ✝ Deus eternus ✝ Eloy ✝
clemens ✝ Heloye ✝ Deus sanctus ✝ Sabaoth ✝ Deus
exercituum Adonay ✝ Deus mirabilis ✝ jao ✝ berax ✝
anepheneton ✝ Deun ineffabilis ✝ Sodoy ✝ Dominatoz
Dominus ✝ on fortissimus ✝ Deus ✝ qui,

the which wouldest be prayed unto of sinners, receive (we be-
siech thee) these sacrifices of praise, and our meek Prayers,
which we unworthy do offer unto thy Divine Majesty. De-
liver us, and have mercy upon us, and prevent with thy Holy
Spirit this work, and with thy blessed help to follow after,
that this our work begun of thee, maybe ended by thy mighty
power; Amen.

Then say this anon after ✝ Homo ✝ sacarus ✝ Mus-
ceolameus ✝ cherubozca ✝ being the figure upon thy
brest aforesaid, the Girdle about thee, the circle made,
bless the Circle with holy Water, and sit down in the
midst, and read this Conjuration as followeth, sitting
back to back at the first time.

I exercise and conjure Baalphares, the practiser and precep-
tor of this Art, by the maker of Heavens and of Earth, and by
his vertue and by his unspeakable Name Tetragrammaton,
and by all the holy Sacraments, and by the holy Majesty and
Deity of the living God. I conjure and exorcise thee Beal-
phares, by the vertue of all Angels, Archangels, Thrones,
Dominations, Principates, Potestates, Virtutes, Cherubim
and Seraphim; and by their vertues, and by the most truest
and speciallest Name of your Master, that you do come unto

THE WORKS OF THE THREE HOLY KINGS

*us, in fair form of man or woman-kinde, here visibly before
this circle; and not terrible by any manner of wayes, This
circle* ['Which must be environed with a goodly company of crosses'] *being our tuition and protection, by the
merciful goodness of our Lord and Saviour Jesus Christ, and
that you do make answer truly, without craft or deceit, unto
all my demands and questions, by the vertue and power of
our Lord Jesus Christ. Amen.*

Scot, *Dis-
covery of
Witchcraft,*
251–53

In this particularly long extract, we are afforded instructions on the conjuration, binding and charging of a spirit.
This operation 'for the inclosing of the said Spirit, and how
to have a true answer of him' represents a distinctly different approach to working with unclean spirits from our
usual manner of speaking about grimoires as whole oper-
ating systems for summoning various spirits from lists or
catalogues. This conjuration of Bealphares is rather more of
a specific rite than a set of practices into which one merely
'plugs' the spirit name and seal, although this is not to
suggest that it bears no resemblances to other more general
techniques of medieval or early modern conjuration.

We also might pull out certain modular operations
within it for other magian rites. The use of Psalms 51
and 22, along with the Pater Noster, Creed and the *Ne nos
inducas*—not to mention the various imprecations for help
by the examples of the Three Noble Kings might well be
employed in consecrations and other rituals.

✝ ✝ ✝

Three Kings in the 'Treatise Sion' of *The Sixth and Seventh Books of Moses*

The following are several (occasionally extended) extracts from this infamous folk magical text. It presents a set of what might be considered 'folk-ceremonial' magical practices drawing upon Hebrew and/or philo-Semitic styles of Christian ritual magic. These include the Laws of Entrance—which presents a whole host of grimoiric tools considered under specific patronage of the Three Holy Kings—as well as various instructions in using the names of the Magi in spirit conjuration.

¶The Vestibule of Entrance
The language and manuscript of this rare and eternal monument of light, and of a higher wisdom, are borrowed from the Cuthans, a tribe of the Samaritans, who were called Cuthim in the Chaldee dialect according to the Talmud, and they were so called in a spirit of derision. They were termed sorcerers because they taught in Cutha, their original place of abode, and afterward in Samaria, the Kabala, or Higher Magic (Book of Kings). Caspar, Melchior, and Balthazar, the chosen archpriests, are shining lights among the Eastern magicians. They were kings and teachers—the first priest/teachers of this glorious knowledge—and from these Samaritans-Cuthans, who were called Nergal according to the traditions of the Talmud, originated the Gypsies,

THE WORKS OF THE THREE HOLY KINGS

who, through degeneracy, lost the consecration of their primordial powers.

¶Laws of Entrance

1. Before you can enter the temple of consecrated light, you must purify your soul and body during thirteen days

2. As a brother and disciple of the new covenant, or as a Christian, you must receive the Holy Sacrament for the glorification of the three kings—Caspar, Melchior, and Balthasar.

3. Three holy masses must be read as often as you make use of this book in your priestly service with your intention fixed upon the three glorified kings.

4. You must provide yourself with a ram's horn, wherewith to call together the angels and spirits. This horn must be included in your intentions of the holy mass.

5. You must wear a breastplate of parchment, ten inches high and ten inches wide, inscribed with the names of the twelve apostles with the five-fold name of Schemhamforasch, in the same order that it is placed on the last leaf [Peter, James, John, Andrew, Philip, Thomas, Bartholomew, Matthew, James, Alpheus, Simon the Canaanite, Judas, Thaddeus, Matthias.]

6. You must draw a circle around you upon white paper, or upon sky blue silk. Its circumference shall be thirteen

A BOOK OF THE MAGI

feet, and at the distance of each foot, one of the following names must be written:

Moseh ⇥⊹⊹⇤ **Messias** ⇥⊹⊹⇤ **Aron** ⇥⊹⊹⇤ **Jehova**
Adonay ⇥⊹⊹⇤ **Jesus** ⇥⊹⊹⇤ **Christus**
Caspar ⇥⊹⊹⇤ **Melchior** ⇥⊹⊹⇤ **Balthasar**
Al ⇥⊹⊹⇤ **Al** ⇥⊹⊹⇤ **Al**

7. Between each name you must place the holy symbol of
   Horet namely:

   ⇥╀ ╀⇤

8. The breastplate must be included in the intention of the
   holy mass.

9. Through consecration with holy triple kings'-water
   and with three burning wax tapers, you must finally
   pronounce a benediction over this book, the horn, the
   breastplate, and the circle, after reading a well-selected
   mysterious ritual.

10. You may enter alone, or begin this great work with two
    companions, by day or by night, but always from the
    first to the thirteenth of the month, and during the
    thirteenth day, and through the whole night of the new
    moon, and also during full moon, when the three plan-
    ets, Saturn, Mars, and Jupiter, are visible in the heavens
    on the day of exorcism, either singly or together.

11. You must always stand with your face toward Zion, or
    toward the rising of the sun.

12. He who refuses a copy of this book, or who suppresses it or steals it, will be seized with eternal trembling, like Cain, and the angels of God will depart from him.

¶Conjuration of the Laws of Moses
Keischu, Nischba, Lawosem—How to be God, so you swore to our parents. Prayer—Eternal of Eternals! Jehovah of Light, Adonay of Truth! Messiah of the All-merciful! Jesus Christ the beloved and All-redemption and love! You have said: Who sees me sees also the Father. Father, eternal Father of the old and new covenant; triune Father, triune Son, triune Spirit, our Father, I beseech and conjure you by the eternal words of your eternal truth. And now the seventeenth chapter of John, or the prayer of Jesus, must be prayed. Closing Prayer of the Conjuration of the Law-Eternal God Jehova, you have said: Ask and it shall be given you. I pray that you may hear your servants Caspar, Melchior, and Balthasar, the arch-priests of your fountain of light! I pray that you may bid your angels to purify me from all sin; that they may breathe upon me in love, and that they may cover me with the shadow of their wings. Send them down! This is my prayer in peace!

¶General Citation of Moses on All Spirits
Adulal! Abulal! Lebusi! Arise and bring before me the spirit N.

Calls with the voice and horn as already known.

A BOOK OF THE MAGI

Here follows the Pentagon, or, the Omnipotent Five-Corners.

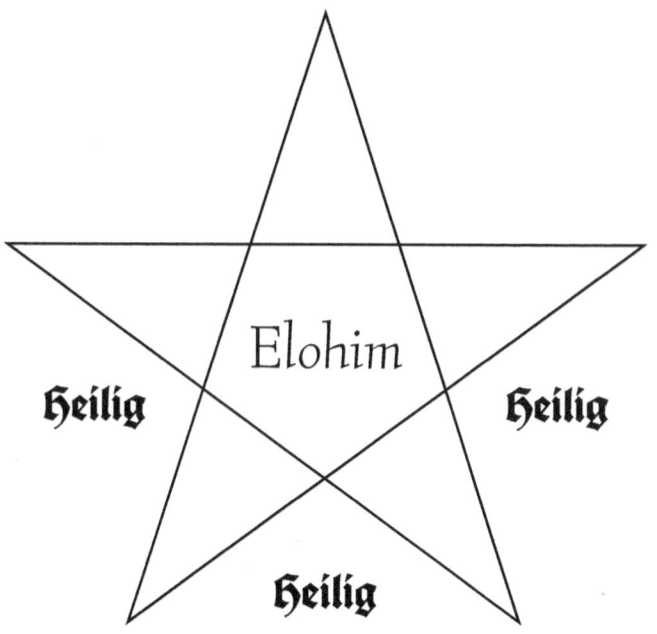

This mysterious figure must be written before the exorcism, in the open air, and in the ground, with consecrated chalk or with the index finger of the right hand dipped in holy three-kings-water, the same as it is written up on the paper, but each line must be thirteen feet in length. The conjuror then kneels in the centre of the star, with uncovered head and with face turned toward Zion, and calls first in a loud voice, coming from the heart, the names of Caspar, Melchior, and Balthasar, thirteen times, and after calling these thirteen times, he

THE WORKS OF THE THREE HOLY KINGS

must also then call the high and sacred name of Elohim 375 times with equal fervor and faith. But only as has already been stated in the Laws of Entrance, No. 10, in the first three days or nights of the new moon, or full moon, or when Saturn, Mars, and Jupiter appear in the heavens.

¶ *Conjurations from* Verus Jesuitarum
  Libellus—*Conjuration II*

I N, servant of God, call, summon, and exorcise you, o Spirit! by the holy apostles and disciples of God, by the holy Evangelists, by St. Matthew, St. Mark, St. Luke, and St. John, and by the three holy men Shadrach, Mesach, and Abednego, and by aU the holy Patriarchs, Prophets, Confessors, Priests, and Levites, and by the chastity of aU the holy virgins, and by the most holy and terrible words: Aphriel, Diefriel, Zada, Zadai, Lamabo, Lamogella, Caratium, Lamogellay, Logim, Lassim lepa, Adeo, Deus, Aleu, Aboy, Aboy, Alon pion dhon, mibizimi, mora, abda, zeud, and by the three holy Magi: Caspar, Melchior, and Balthasar, and by that which Solomon, Manasses, Agrippa, and Cyprian knew and exorcised the spirits and by the ascension of Christ into the highest realms of peace, that you appear before me in a beautiful affable, and human form, and bring me (from the depths of the seas) N. million of the best Spanish gold without any disturbance, or else I will damn you body and soul, abstaining wholly from all harm, without noise, lightning, or tempest, without terror and trembling, and place yourself before me outside this circle. And this I command you by the most

93

A BOOK OF THE MAGI

Peterson (ed.), *Sixth and Seventh Books*, 258–59

holy Mother of God Mary, and by all the merits of the principal Martyrs of God.

||||||||||||||||||||||||||||||||||||||||||||||||||||||||||||||||||||||||||||||||||||||||||||||||

Work of Dominating Authorities

The following work is very much built upon my study of traditional Hoodoo and related folk magical methodologies, chiefly of course African-American Conjure and Latin American folk magic, and my discussion with professional rootworkers and Hoodooists.[119] While the Three Kings do not tend to make huge appearance or impact in English-speaking Hoodoo, they are certainly present in Hispanic traditions—for many of the reasons outlined above—and American botanicas can stock Los Tres Reyes incenses (typically in multicoloured resins) and sometimes even oils. There is even a Dutch brand of Three Kings charcoal briquettes, popular for burning frankincense and myrrh upon

This working employs *inter alia* dirts from relevant locations—as with the street dust and the older *eulogiae* traditions—as well as the infamous Psalm 72:10–11, understood to reference the Gifts and Adoration of the Magi, used as a charm in psalm magic for works of dominating authorities. Finally, the insertion of the packet into the shoe to 'step

---

119 I am especially grateful to my friend Professor Charles Porterfield for the many hours of fascinating and edifying conversation about these matters, and look forward to many more in the future.

THE WORKS OF THE THREE HOLY KINGS

on' combines the magically potent travelling and obeisant kneeling of the Magi.

¶All Kings Shall Bow Domination Working
Take image of target, turn upside down, and cross it with the names of the Three Kings, written 12 times. Sprinkle dirt from a Nativity scene, especially from around where the Kings kneel, over the image. Cover it with a King of Spades playing card, face down. Prop a lithograph of the Three Kings and the Star (or, alternatively, The Star card from the Tarot) up against a pillar candle. Fix the candle with frankincense, myrrh, and gold, and dress it and the image in Domination and/ or Essence of Bend Over Oil. Burn the candle atop the image of your target. Line up three white candles carved with names of the Three Kings and dressed in Three Kings Oil. Stand them atop the other three King cards from a playing card deck, face up. Pray Psalm 72:10–13. At conclusion, 'bow' the candles by putting them out upside down, intoning each name as you do. Fold the target's image into a small packet and wear it in your shoe, stepping on them as you move forward.

||||||||||||||||||||||||||||||||||||||||||||||||||||||||||||||||||||||||||||||||||||||||||

Works of Adoration

This final section includes a variety of my own operations, adapted from historical sources and customs, as well as contemporary practices, finally mediated through divination and spiritwork.

A BOOK OF THE MAGI

¶Consecrations

The Folger Vb.26 manuscript contains a familiar talismanic design dedicated to the Magi.[120]

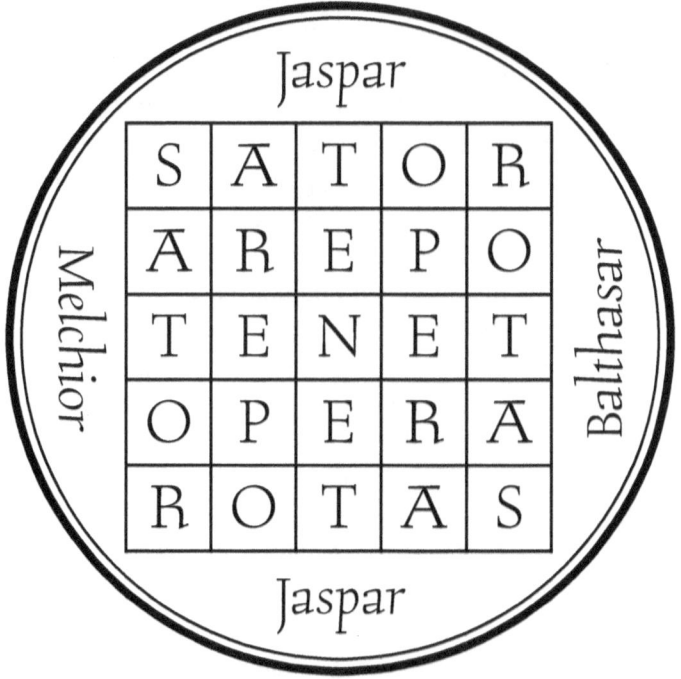

Obviously, the infamous SATOR square is by no means unique to this seal. It does suggest however that other workings with the square—and there are many!—might be conducted under the auspices of the Magi. While the seal is presented as a talisman of protection, and can certainly

---

120 This seal is found in the Shakespeare Library Folger MS Vb.26. It can be found in *Book of Oberon*, ed. by Daniel Harms, James R. Clark and Joseph H. Peterson (Woodbury: Llewellyn, 2015), 372.

be used in that manner, I have found it can also serve as a means to consecrate one's *materia* and objects sacred to the Three Kings.

I also recommend painting this upon a dedicated plate, perhaps in a gold paint. This may then be used to make offerings, perform workings, and charge talismanic objects. The following operation is a simple consecration I came up with that I have found effective:

> Place the object or materials to be consecrated atop the Three Kings Seal on a plate. Lay a circle of rue around the edge of the plate, clockwise for works of harmony, discovery, or devotion and anti-clockwise for works of disruption or avoidance. As you sprinkle the rue, contemplate the Journey. Lay another circle inside the first, this time of hyssop, and this time meditate upon the Adoration. Burn three candles, each carved with one of the names + CASPAR + BALTHAZAR + MEL-CHIOR +, around the object being consecrated. Pray Psalm 72 (especially verse 10–13). Recite Matthew 2:1–12 if you wish. Pray Psalm 51 and 22. Let the candles burn down.

As you develop a stock of materials—incenses, oils, powders, dirts, etc.—you may wish to add these to the consecration.

¶Basic Supplies
Here are a few basic formulae used for anything related to the Three Kings and working with the Magi, most widely conceived as the collective magic-using dead. They are reports from personal operations, and should be taken as suggestions for developing one's own practice, rather than

A BOOK OF THE MAGI

historical accounts or formulary. Certainly Three Kings incense—as mentioned above, this is usually small nuggets of multi-coloured resin/s—can also be bought at most botanicas. I would still advise consecrating it oneself by some method you find effective and suitable.

Three Kings Water

Collect holy water from a church on Epiphany. If able, find a priest to bless the water personally. Take home, or to a three-way crossroads, and consecrate, either in the manner outlined above or by your own customs.[121]

Some modern magicians and witches seem to consider that the collection of holy water from a church must necessarily be a thing of secret, subterfuge, and larceny. While the theft of various materials from a church can indeed be a potent empowerment of said materia, it should also be noted that this is not a requirement. Nor is it my personal experience of any Italian-American Catholic church I have visited, although obviously this may vary from parish to parish. I have consistently found that priests and parishioners alike are delighted that you take away and employ holy water. It is for using after all, about the home and elsewhere, and has plenty of applications that do not require you to explain your sorcerous endeavours to strangers or clergy.

---

121 You may perhaps wish to include various blessings or exorcisms of water, such as can be found in Philip T. Weller, ed., *The Roman Ritual: In Latin and English With Rubrics and Plainchant Notation*, 3 vols. (Boonville: Preserving Christian Publications, 2007).

THE WORKS OF THE THREE HOLY KINGS

A Three Kings Oil

On Epiphany add gold, frankincense, and myrrh to olive or sweet almond oil. Consecrate.

You may wish to include the Blessing of the Oil from the Roman Ritual, which I include here.

Blessing of Oil

P: Our help is in the name of the Lord.
All: Who made heaven and earth.

Exorcism of the Oil

God's creature, oil, I cast out the demon from you by God the Father + almighty, who made heaven and earth and sea, and all that they contain. Let the adversary's power, the devil's legions, and all Satan's attacks and machinations be dispelled and driven afar from this creature, oil. Let it bring health in body and mind to all who use it, in the name of God + the Father almighty, and of our Lord Jesus + Christ, His Son, and of the Holy Spirit, the Advocate, as well as in the love of the same Jesus Christ our Lord, who is coming to judge both the living and the dead and the world by fire.

All: Amen.
P: O Lord, heed my prayer.
All: And let my cry come unto you.
P: The Lord be with you.
All: And with your spirit.

Let us pray.
Lord God almighty, before whom the hosts of angels

A BOOK OF THE MAGI

stand in awe, and whose heavenly service we acknowledge; may it please you to regard favorably and to bless + and hallow + this creature, oil, which by your power has been pressed from the juice of olives. You have ordained it for anointing the sick, so that, when they are made well, they may give thanks to you, the living and true God. Grant, we pray, that those who will use this oil, which we are blessing + in your name, may be delivered from all suffering, all infirmity, and all wiles of the enemy. Let it be a means of averting any kind of adversity from man, made in your image and redeemed by the precious blood of your Son, so that he may never again suffer the sting of the ancient serpent; through Christ our Lord. All: Amen.

It is sprinkled with holy water.[122]

I also recommend exploring and experimenting with other prayers for blessing and sanctifying oil, including other Scriptural references, prayers for anointing and healing.[123]

A Three Kings Incense
On Epiphany compound frankincense and myrrh. Various recipes also instruct adding benzoin, sandalwood, aloeswood, or copal. My recommendation is to take this to divination and ascertain which ingredients work best for you, but I would also counsel sticking to a trinity of ingredients,

---

122 See *Roman Ritual*. For an online source, see http://vultuschristi.org/index.php/2010/01/the-blessing-of-oil-in-the-roman-ritual/. Last accessed 30 December 2017.
123 For instance, http://dategodnme.blogspot.co.uk/2011/07/prayer-blessing-of-anointing-oil.html. Last accessed 30 December 2017.

at least for a first attempt. Consecrate. Pray an Exorcism of the Incense:

O God of Abraham, God of Isaac, God of Jacob, deign to bless these odoriferous spices so that they may receive strength, virtue, and power to attract the Good Spirits, and to banish and cause to retire all hostile Phantoms. Through Thee, O Most Holy ADONAI, Who livest and reignest unto the Ages of the Ages. Amen.

I exorcise thee, O Spirit impure and unclean, thou who art a hostile Phantom, in the Name of God, that thou quit this Perfume, thou and all thy deceits, that it may be consecrated and sanctified in the name of God Almighty. May the Holy Spirit of God grant protection and virtue unto those who use these Perfumes; and may the hostile and evil Spirit and Phantom never be able to enter therein, through the Ineffable Name of God Almighty. Amen.

O Lord, deign to bless and to sanctify this Creature of Perfume so that it may be a remedy unto mankind for the health of body and of soul, through the Invocation of Thy Holy Name. May all Creatures who receive the odour of this incense and of these spices receive health of body and of soul, through Him Who hath formed the Ages. Amen.

A Three Kings Chalk

Take three pieces of chalk and baptise them in the names of the Three Kings with holy water, with Three Kings Water being best. Grind them to dust with blessed salt. Add a

A BOOK OF THE MAGI

small amount of infusion of rue, as well as frankincense
and myrrh oils. Shape the wet mass into three sticks of
new Three Kings chalk. Consecrate. Pray a Blessing of the
Chalk:

> Loving God, bless this chalk which you have created,
> that it may be helpful to your people; and grant that
> through the invocation of your most Holy Name that we
> who use it in faith to write upon the door of our home
> the names of your holy ones Caspar, Melchior, and
> Balthazar, may receive health of body and protection
> of soul for all who dwell in or visit our home; through
> Jesus Christ our Lord. Amen.[124]

A Three Kings Ink
Add frankincense and myrrh oil and gold (in metal or
alchemical oil form) to ink purchased or made in the hour
and day of Mercury. Add a few drops of your own blood,
ideally three, preferably taken from the little finger of the
left hand. Consecrate. Pray an Orison of the Ink:

> I exorcise thee, O Creature of Ink, by ANAIRETON, by
> SIMULATOR, and by the Name ADONAI, and by the
> Name of Him through Whom all things were made, that
> thou be unto me an aid and succour in all things which I
> wish to perform by thine aid.

---

124 As an additional magian significance, this blessing is taken from a Carmelite presentation of a prayer specifically designed for the blessing of chalk used to mark the
C+M+B of a house blessing on Epiphany. The entire rite can be found at: http://www.
carmelites.net/news/chalking-door-epiphany-house-blessing-2015/. Last accessed 30
December 2017.

THE WORKS OF THE THREE HOLY KINGS

The following are two simple additional tools that can be constructed once you have at least some of the above supplies.

A Travelling Oil

Add rue to olive oil. Add three small bundles of camel hair, tied with virgin thread that has been soaked in Three Kings Oil. Consecrate. Pray suitable orisons Anoint with 3 crosses on your feet or shoes. Use for safe travel, protection, and against tiredness—especially on journeys.

Owing to the ease with which fresh herbs can spoil oils, I recommend using three generous pinches of dried rue. If you are having trouble sourcing authentic camel hair, consider looking for the bristles of fancy paintbrushes.

Ribbons of the Magi

Take (preferably white silk) ribbons and write the names of the Three Kings in Three Kings Ink. It may be written with a stylus, brush or pen of hazel, cypress, or rosemary handle. If it can be written with the pen or quill of a dead magician, it is better. When you wish to empower a talisman with particular persistence, endurance, or far-reaching potency wrap it in these ribbons. You can also use these as bookmarks to empower the incantations marked.

Using the ribbons of the travelling operations for other purposes might seem inappropriate, but I welcome you to consider the journey of the consecrated object or materia itself.

A BOOK OF THE MAGI

A Bag of the Adoration

On Epiphany, take a white silk bag and place inside gold, frankincense, and myrrh. As you place these items in the bag, declare: *as the Magi adored the Christ Child, so are these gifts given to the glory of Son known by the Star in the East.* Pray. Invoke and cross + CASPAR + BALZATHAR + MELCHIOR + Tie it shut and hang three king charms from the knot. Smoke it in Three Kings incense and feed it Three Kings oil. You now have a talismanic representation of the authority of the Anointed One as well as a Star to call the Magi.

The king charms mentioned can be crown charms, or could be elaborately carved king figurines, or even small Christmas tree decorations of the kings. For various reasons I prefer using king chess-piece charms.

A Crown of the Magi

Take a bath of rosemary and bay, with frankincense and myrrh essential oils, for three days. On the third day, which should be a day of Mercury, in the hour of Mercury take white and/or gold (preferably virgin) thread soaked in Three Kings (and other appropriate) Oil/s and wrap rosemary stalks into a crown wreath. Weave in bay leaves, which can bear the three names written in Three Kings ink with a pen or quill of the nature discussed above. Wrap it in Ribbons of the Magi. Do all this in the name of the Three Kings. Burn a white or gold candle dressed in Three Kings Oil and drip wax over the thread binding. Pray Psalm 51, and declare:

THE WORKS OF THE THREE HOLY KINGS

> *As the Three Kings ventured by the light of the Star in the East for knowledge of the True way and the King of Kings, so too may I wear the Crown of the Magi as I search for wisdom.*

Wear the Crown when you are studying magic or searching for something.

I have found this Crown assists in divination (a form of searching, after all), as well as performing these sorts of magian operations. If you wished to make this a more involved working, one could bathe for twelve days before beginning the operation.

I can also recommend making and gifting three of these Crowns as offerings—given on your altar or left at a place associated with the Magi. The Three Kings were traditionally conceived of as meeting at a three-way crossroads, for instance.

A Magi Shrine or Altar

A suitable image, statuary or icon for the Three Kings, preferably one gifted to you by an older magician. Images of important occult philosophers and magical practitioners, enshrined in the manner given above. Three Kings workings, *materia*, and tools, along with those of a dead magician. An incense burner and at least one cup for offering libations of wine, at least one candlestick for candle offerings, and perhaps a vase for flowers. You may keep any of your magical equipment—tools and talismans and so on— that you wish to be empowered by the Magi here.

A BOOK OF THE MAGI

Statuary or images pertinent to your working tradition/s that govern or lend patronage to particular forms of magic you are employing—including both Christian and pagan figures responsible for matters like divination, healing, protection, or cursing—offer further coherence points and stability to particular spirit contact and workings: an icon of Hippocrates or Asclepius on one's Magi altar if one works a lot of healing magic and medicine, for instance. Such working of an icon utilises not simply an ancestral veneration of that ancient physician directly or solely (although these icons can also clearly form points for access to such devotional and religious praxis), but a forebear and figurehead of a broad inclusive historical lineage of doctors. A lineage with an oath to which medieval astrologer-physicians and even some early modern cunning-folk may have felt some sense of affinity or allegiance. Like the Prayers to the Elementals, we come closer to the spirits we wish to work with by worshipping *like* them, in parallel facing the same vision of the divine, with comparable goals and methodologies.

Similarly, at least one icon of a psychopomp or a hero who has undergone a katabasis provides useful *loci* by which to facilitate smooth spirit contact with the dead. This figure can also inform how one might call to the Magi—Orpheus' patronage of music and poetry is a particularly apt one, for instance.

Other iconography might include (tasteful!) depictions of skulls, skeletons and souls—the heraldry of the dead. This heraldry also extends to their flora. Necromantic botanicals (such as bay, dandelion, rosemary, acacia, yew, cypress, and so on) as well as exorcist plant allies (like hyssop, Solomon's seal, devil's shoe string, and so many others)

THE WORKS OF THE THREE HOLY KINGS

might all be kept on a Magi altar, hung, scattered, and bundled into talismans.

It is entirely appropriate to keep items of devotion to necromantic saints on and around a magian altar. Lazarus is an obvious example of this category, of course, but so are saints such as Rosalia and Stephen, whose posthumous cults came to prominence when their bones were discovered via the directions given by holy apparitions. As Williamson noted, altars dedicated to the Magi were especially common in churches of saints considered relatives of the Holy Family—such as Martha, Mary Magdalene, Anne, and so on. If you have an altar to Saint Cyprian and work sorcery with him, consider having this Magi altar above or near Cyprian. The altar may, for instance, be mounted on a shelf with icons hung on the walls. I should note that I have been told that in *curanderismo* traditions Cipriano is regarded as not only capable but likely to knock over items, especially statues, placed above him, with the exceptions of icons of Jesus or the archangels. As somewhat of a traditional 'work-around', icons actually hung on a wall above Cipriano are usually considered more behind him than above him.

Similarly, consider carving, painting, chalking, or otherwise marking the names of the Magi on *any* altar upon which you work magic: not as a dedication of ownership by the Kings, but a place to begin, return to, and begin again one's pilgrimages and holy magic. As the altarcloth upon a holy altar is sometimes considered representative of the shroud of Christ, the altar is itself a tomb. As the Bible is placed upon the altar, so is it understood as the Word of God born into the world, and is thus simultaneously the manger. These are of course mysteries with profound necromantic significances. Practitioners with a focus on dead

A BOOK OF THE MAGI

magicians, lineage ancestors, saints and Madonnas, and related devotions and nigromancies should feel empowered to explore within their own practices the mythic connections and relationships that present themselves through their own folk necromancy of the Magi.

Celebrate the birthdays of your magician forebears and other dates significant to the history of your magic. Light candles, call your tutelary ancestors and offer wine and/or water before any serious operations of divination or sorcery. Hang roots from threads and dry herbs to be used for magical operations. Keep books of magic you are working and studying on this altar. Store oils, baths, and other experiments. Brew spiritual baths at this space, asking for the power of the Magi to imbue your infusions and decoctions with the necessary virtues. Conduct your scrying experiments here. Make petitions to be granted access to more resources for working your craft, or for protection in your journeys, or for dominating a figure of authority. Of course, given the Three Kings' attested abilities to observe and interpret heavenly signs, they can provide useful tuition in astrological matters. Ask for their wisdom and clarity when divining in front of them.

CONCLUSIONS

In this volume of lore, prayer, and spellcraft I have sought to present history, devotion, and magic; that is, tradition, myth, and the sorcerous application of both.

My appeal to tradition here is not intended to quash or lambast innovation and experimentation in one's personal practice in the slightest, but rather comes from the journey of my own Magi work that has lead me to connect more deeply with the shades of my predecessor magicians, astrologers, cunning-folk, conjurers, and pilgrims who have also looked to the Three Kings. Mine is not simply a practice built around calling upon Caspar, Melchior, and Balthazar as three patron saints, but rather the praxis itself of a coherence of distant powerful magicians about a common Star, Journey, and Adoration. A Star in the East of prophecy and power, announcing the coming of Light in the Darkness. A Journey across time, space, and the veil of tears to impart new joy. An Adoration of the Light of Life, both pointing to that which we kneel before and grasping the means to secure and extend that light. Tradition and history for me are not a stick with which to Slaughter the Innocence of invention, but I hope a Star to light our way to something greater. We stand upon the shoulders of our ancestors and, occasionally, they ride upon ours: from their struggles across deserts, to the wisdom of their art and foresight, and

A BOOK OF THE MAGI

the riches of their bones and gifts. For me, the Magi thus form as a necromantic locus of the spirits of what might be called in other traditions the Mighty Dead: ancestor magicians of many colours, creeds, and culti.

You may have noticed a lack of meditation upon the etymology of the word *Magi*, or of a scarcity of collected exegetic material on the significances of their Gifts. Firstly, I assure you this is deliberate. Secondly, I humbly suggest that there are countless resources available from the last two thousand years, which you should feel emboldened to research. Indeed, thirdly, I actively encourage you to explore and integrate this research into your own meditations, devotions, and sorceries.

In putting this book together I have come to a fresh appreciation of the idea of the wisdom in recognising and serving something greater than oneself. For me a folk necromancy of the Magi is not simply about kneeling before Christ, but of finding a Child of Light in what we wisely chose to honour and celebrate, and in the journey of life with all of its travels and travails. As I have pointed out several times, the Magi are not explicitly understood to be prostrating themselves before Christ's Divinity, but as offering pilgrimage and gifts to His Majesty—to the wisdom of good rulership. The continual notion of the power gained through service is less a paradox than a humming of a hymn upon that potent tension.

I leave you with what I have gleaned of their messages so far: be joyful in your travels, though travails they may be. Prepare for your epiphanies with an eye on both the horizon and where you have come from. Meet your fellows at a three-way crossroads, and bring gifts.

BIBLIOGRAPHY

PRIMARY SOURCES

Agrippa, Heinrich Cornelius. *Three Books of Occult Philosophy*. London, 1651.

Book of Oberon, ed. by Daniel Harms, James R. Clark and Joseph H. Peterson. Woodbury: Llewellyn, 2015.

d'Auzoles Lapeyre, Jacques. *L'Epiphanie, ou Pensées nouvelles à la Gloire de Dieu touchant les trois Mages*. Paris, 1638.

de Mornay, Philippe. *A Woorke concerning the trewnesse of the Christian Religion*. London, 1587.

The Grimoire of Arthur Gauntlet, ed. by David Rankine. London: Avalonia, 2011.

Grimoire of Honorius, ed. by David Rankine and Paul Harry Barron. London: Avalonia, 2013.

Scot, Reginald. *Discoverie of Witchcraft*. London, 1584; 1665 edition.

SECONDARY SOURCES

Barthel, Peter, and George van Kooten, eds. *The Star of Bethlehem and the Magi: Interdisciplinary Perspectives from Experts on the Ancient Near East, the Greco-Roman World, and Modern Astronomy*. Leiden: Brill, 2015.

Black, George F. 'Scottish Charms and Amulets'. *Proceedings of the Society of Antiquaries of Scotland* 27 (1892–93).

Boardman, S., J. Davies, and Eila Williamson, eds. *Saints' Cults in the Celtic World*. Woodbridge: Boydell, 2008.

Boffey, Julia. '"Many grete myraclys...in divers contreys of the eest": The Reading and Circulation of the Middle English Prose *Three Kings of Cologne*', in *Medieval Women: Texts and Contexts in Late Medieval Britain. Essays for Felicity Riddy*, ed. J. Wogan-Browne *et al.* (Brepols: Turnhout, 2000), 35–47.

Buhler. Stephen M. 'Marsilio Ficino's *De stella magorum* and Renaissance Views of the Magi', *Renaissance Quarterly* 43.2 (Summer, 1990): 348–71.

Caldwell. D. H. *Angels, Nobles and Unicorns. Art and Patronage in Medieval Scotland*. Edinburgh, 1982.

Callander, J. Graham. 'Fourteenth-century Brooches and other Ornaments in the National Museum of Antiquities of Scotland'. *Proceedings of the Society of Antiquaries of Scotland* 58 (1923/24): 160–84.

Crossed Keys. Dover: Scarlet Imprint, 2011.

Deery, Mary B. *Medieval Ring Brooches in Ireland: A Study of Jewellry, Dress and Society*. Wicklow: Bray, Co., 1998.

The Encyclopedia of Religions, ed. M. Eliade (New York, 1987).

Ettlinger, Ellen. 'British Amulets in London Museums', *Folklore* 50 (1939).

The Complete Harley Manuscript 2253: Volume 3, ed. and trans. Susanna Fein with David Raybin and Jan Ziolkowski. Western Michigan University: Medieval Institute Publications, 2015.

Hull, Vida J. 'Spiritual Pilgrimage in the Paintings of Hans Memling', in *Art and Architecture of Late Medieval Pil-*

grimage, ed. Sarah Blick and Rita Tekippe (Leiden: Brill, 2004).

Hutton, Ronald. *Stations of the Sun: A History of the Ritual Year in Britain*. Oxford: Oxford University Press, 2001.

McNally, R. 'The Three Holy Kings in Early Irish Latin Writing', in *Kyriakon: Festschrift Johannes Quasten*, eds. P. Granfield and J. Jungmann. Münster/Westf., 1970.

Mitchell, Shelagh. 'Richard II: Kingship and the Cult of the Saints', in *The Regal Image of Richard II and the Wilton Diptych*, ed. Dillian Gordon, Lisa Monnas and Caroline M. Barron (London: Harvey Miller, 1997).

Mountney, Hugh. *The Three Holy Kings of Cologne: How They Journeyed from Persia to Cologne and Their Veneration in England*. Leominster: Gracewing, 2003.

Peterson, Joseph H. *Sixth and Seventh Books of Moses*. Lake Worth: Ibis Press, 2008.

Rahmani, L. Y. 'The Adoration of the Magi on Two Sixth-Century CE Eulogia Tokens', *Israel Exploration Journal* 29.1 (1979).

Spencer, Brian. *Pilgrims Souvenirs and Secular Badges*. London, 1998.

Toy, Barbara. *Travelling the Incense Route: From Arabia to the Levant in the Footsteps of the Magi*. London: I. B. Tauris, 2009.

Trexler, Richard C. *The Journey of the Magi: Meanings in History of a Christian Story*. Princeton: Princeton University Press, 1997.

Webb, Diana. *Pilgrims and Pilgrimages in the Medieval West*. New York: I. B. Tauris, 1999.

¶FURTHER WORKS

As both an author for and editor of the Folk Necromancy in Transmission series, I am proud to be part of Revelore Press, and you should certainly check us out at:

http://revelore.press

If you are interested in my writings on the Magi, on folk necromancy, and on magic and history in general, you can find my bloggery (along with recordings and notices of my talks, classes and webinars) at:

http://www.alexandercummins.com

I keep a storehouse of early modern texts on magic and medicine at:

http://grimoiresontape.tumblr.com.

I can be also be found on Instagram and Twitters:

@grimoiresontape

My podcast, Radio Free Golgotha, which I co-host with the eponymous Goat Jesse Hathaway Diaz of Wolf & Goat, can be found at:

https://radio-free-golgotha.squarespace.com

You can also come chat at our Folk Necromancy forum, if you are on those Facebooks, at:

https://www.facebook.com/groups/folknecromancy

¶ABOUT THIS SERIES

The Folk Necromancy in Transmission series examines the folk magical expressions and interrelations of the histories, philosophies, and practices of spirit conjuration, ghost-lore, eschatology, charm-craft, demonology, and the mass of rituals, protocols, and beliefs signalled by the terms 'nigromancy', 'necromancy' and their various equivalents in traditions across the world.

Here we take the canonical and reveal the folkloric expression; here the historical text inspires new practice and discourse. This series will not simply chart the print history of grimoires, or their socio-political context, but explore their actual magical usage. Within this exploration comes discourse on and with those traditions, extant or extinct, deemed 'necromantic' that are passed through oral transmission.

Raising the dead, we acknowledge the raising of necromancy itself, for it is still the breath of the reader that gives new life to the Dead from the bones of old Books. This is a folk necromancy that is at once extant and revived, inspired and yet-to-be. Here we walk hand-in-hand with the patrons of this particular Art.

¶ABOUT THE AUTHOR

Alexander Cummins is a consultant sorcerer, professional diviner, and trained historian as well as a devotee of the Magi. He holds a doctorate in the history of early modern British magic from the University of Bristol. He is the co-founder and editor of the Folk Necromancy in Transmission series for Revelore Press and co-host of the Radio Free Golgotha podcast.

Dr Cummins has published on topics including planetary sorcery, prophecy and apocalypse, transatlantic folk magic, the material history of talismanic objects, occult herbalism, the cut-up technique of Burroughs and Gysin, and, not least, Saint Cyprian.

Cummins writes for both academic and esoteric publishers, facilitates a range of workshops and lecture series, teaches in community spaces and virtual classrooms alike, consults privately with clients and organisations, and speaks at a wide variety of events. speaks at a wide variety of events. The good doctor lectures on topics such as astrological magic, geomancy, humoural theory, grimoires, and of course folk necromancy. He is currently based in Brooklyn, where he lives with his amazing wife and their vast expanse of cat.

¶ABOUT THIS VOLUME

In this third release of *Folk Necromancy in Transmission*, series editor, author, and magician Dr Alexander Cummins guides us through the traditions, context, and magic of the Three Kings, offering in parallel his own gifts as an historian and sorcerer.

This book presents the history, folklore, myth, cult and culture of the biblical Magi from their first appearances in ceremonial funerary art to their role in the colonisation of the so-called 'New World' and facets of their worldwide cult of devotion.

This book follows (in) the footprints of the Magi throughout the grimoiric records to present the magical operations and rites dedicated to these figures. This magian devotional also contains new rituals, talismans, and methodologies from the author's own practice.

This understanding of historical research and practice as two pillars of a specific necromancy of magic seeks to celebrate and explore the fullness of our relationship with the magic texts of the past, in tandem with the magicians of the past. The Magi transform the magician, not as the recipients of devotion solely, but as guides and ancestors in our search for our Star...

¹ CUM ERGO NATUS esset Iesus in Bethleem Iudaeae in diebus Herodis regis ecce magi ab oriente venerunt Hierosolymam

² dicentes ubi est qui natus est rex Iudaeorum vidimus enim stellam eius in oriente et venimus adorare eum

³ audiens autem Herodes rex turbatus est et omnis Hierosolyma cum illo

⁴ et congregans omnes principes sacerdotum et scribas populi sciscitabatur ab eis ubi Christus nasceretur

⁵ at illi dixerunt ei in Bethleem Iudaeae sic enim scriptum est per prophetam

⁶ et tu Bethleem terra Iuda nequaquam minima es in principibus Iuda ex te enim exiet dux qui reget populum meum Israhel

⁷ tunc Herodes clam vocatis magis diligenter didicit ab eis tempus stellae quae apparuit eis

⁸ et mittens illos in Bethleem dixit ite et interrogate diligenter de puero et cum inveneritis renuntiate mihi ut et ego veniens adorem eum

⁹ qui cum audissent regem abierunt et ecce stella quam viderant in oriente antecedebat eos usque dum veniens staret supra ubi erat puer

¹⁰ videntes autem stellam gavisi sunt gaudio magno valde

[11] et intrantes domum invenerunt puerum cum Maria matre eius et procidentes adoraverunt eum et apertis thesauris suis obtulerunt ei munera aurum tus et murram

[12] et responso accepto in somnis ne redirent ad Herodem per aliam viam reversi sunt in regionem suam

[10] reges Tharsis et insulae munera offerent reges Arabiae et Saba tributum conferent

[11] et adorabunt eum omnes reges universae nationes servient ei

[12] quia eruet pauperem a potente et inopem cui non est adiutor

[13] parcet inopi et pauperi et animas pauperum salvabit

A Book of the Magi was typeset in Kingfisher
(Jeremy Tankard), Robinson (Greg Gazdowicz),
Miniscule (Thomas Huot-Marchand), RTF
Stern Pro (Jim Rimmer), & ALOT Deutsche
Schrift (Rudolf Koch).

www.ingramcontent.com/pod-product-compliance
Lightning Source LLC
Chambersburg PA
CBHW021155080526
44588CB00008B/342